DEDICATION

A Gift of Love from the Cosmos to Humankind

D1595888

TABLE OF CONTENTS

Acknowledgements   vii

Preface   ix

Introduction   13

1. Choosing to Begin a Mystical Path   19

2. From Chakras & Subtle Energy
      to Healing & Miracles   25

3. Background to the Enlightenment Vision   34

4. Enlightenment Vision   47

5. The Threshold of Christ-Consciousness   51

6. The Lessons Continue   59

7. Healing with the Seven Rays   72

8. My Father's Death & the
      Descent of Consciousness   79

9. Life as Lessons in Self-Realization   85

10. Lessons in Higher Consciousness   97

11. Incarnation – Embodying Divine Presence   118

12. Transition on all Levels:
      Moving to Washington, DC   139

13. Mystical Interlude of Miracles   149

14. Mornings with the Masters   155

15. Humanity, Divinity, and Wholeness   172

16. Consciousness: Experienced, Explained,
      & Expanded   191

17. Living the "I AM" Presence   212

18: The Tao of Blessing Others   221

ACKNOWLEDGEMENTS

First, I must acknowledge the Ascended Masters who work with me (and on me!), without whom there would be no reason for this book: Lady Quan Yin, Paramahansa Yogananda, Jesus Christ, Mother Mary, Mary Magdalene, Lord Buddha, Master Lao Tzu, and High Priest Melchizedek. Until recently, I mostly recognized seven Ascended Masters as teaching me, but, I recently recognized that Master Lao Tzu has taught me as well, so now there are eight.

Among human beings, I am most grateful to those who serve on the Board of Directors of the Self-Realization Community for their support in naming this book the first publication of the Self-Realization Community, including Sepideh Saiedi, my beautiful soul sister, and the truly efficient and intelligent Chloe Sedlak, whose mother also deserves great credit and my gratitude for copy-editing this book. I am also thankful to the SRC board for allowing me to use the beautiful logo created for us by Tyne Lowe, as well as to Tyne for listening to my description of several visions, and creating art to express these visions!

Of course, I am grateful to my family for their support: my parents, Dick and Joy Dodson, for their incredible spiritual legacy, their life-long example of service, their generous support, and especially how much my father appreciated my theological writing and believed in me;

my sister, Janet, for taking care of our parents' health, finances, and so on, so that I could focus on starting a new spiritual community and write books; my amazing daughter, Christina, for her love, wise judgement, and support; my niece, Shantala, for her intelligent ideas and multi-faceted support; my brother, Dave, who believes in me – the best gift I can ask for and am grateful to be receiving, for it warms my heart; and also, I am grateful for my son, Clint, who is a brilliant physicist and old soul who helped me clarify my perspective on quantum physics, and who did his best to shed scientific light onto my limited understanding of the complexities of physics.

Finally, I would like to thank the Seven Archangels of the Seven Rays: Archangel Michael, Archangel Jophiel, Archangel Chamuel, Archangel Gabriel, Archangel Raphael, Archangel Uriel, and Archangel Zadkiel, as well as my own guardian angels and all the angels of love and light who assist me with healing sessions. Without the angels, nothing would really work well in this universe!

PREFACE

On one level, this book is the story of how to lose your mind without going crazy. As someone who feels very fond of rational thought, scientific inquiry, and logical deduction, I often felt as though I were either going crazy, or must already be crazy during the development of the mystical side of my "Self." Mystical journeys require courage, as one has to let go of many familiar intellectual landmarks along with the comfort of rational moorings in the mind.

I invite you to find your inner courage in order to explore the realities of mystical journeys, both my own, as well as your own. I invite you to choose courage, rather than needing to resort to skepticism, which may, at times, be helpful on journeys of faith, but which can impede journeys in the realm of the mystical mind.

On this level, then, this book is the story of my journey from rational religious person and scientific skeptic, to explorer and meditator on an Eastern spiritual path, to mystic with full-blown connections to Higher Beings, including various Ascended Masters.

On another level, this book is the story of these various Ascended Masters seeking to "disciple" a new generation of mystics and masters in this post-modern world.

Even the Ascended Masters have admitted to me that, while they walked the earth, they never had to deal with anything like the cyber realities that distract us intimately and constantly via multiple technologies throughout our days *and* our nights. Nor did they have to deal with the multiple sources of toxic pollution and human-made poor diet that are now threatening the physical, mental, and spiritual health of so many of us human beings. Nor did they usually have to deal with a break in the traditional transmission of spiritual teachings from embodied (or incarnate) master to disciple.

Most of us in this world today have no Self-Realized Master to whom we can turn by driving or walking down the street to seek today's dose of teachings on the subject of Enlightenment. Most of us do not know where to go to learn about attaining higher spiritual consciousness, unless we choose to travel to India, or Nepal, or Tibet. Most of us do not have an Enlightened Master who is part of our daily lives. We may wonder at whose feet we can sit in order to learn to let go of ego and to develop into Self-Realized Masters ourselves.

We need to be able to access guidance from people with Enlightened Consciousness. Yes, we may find them in books and online, but an ongoing, conscious communication is needed as well.

If we cannot access Fully Enlightened Masters in person, then we need to be able to access the Ascended Masters who can teach us directly from higher realms. This book therefore shares the path that has led me to receiving teachings directly from seven Ascended Masters, in order to encourage you to pursue a similar path yourself.

A note to feminists (myself included!): for a long time I resisted using simply the term "Masters," as it is, in its origins, an exclusively masculine term. The trouble is that, in the twenty-first century we have largely inherited, at the very least, many androcentric linguistic practices and, at the worst, decidedly sexist usages of language.

For instance, I could refer to Ascended Masters and Ascended Mistresses, but in the English language, the feminine equivalent of "masters" has obviously acquired derogatory connotations, which would fail suitably to describe these sacred Beings.

Often, individual female Ascended Masters are referred to as "Lady" or by some form of the name "mother." Because their names or forms of address honor them individually as *feminine* sacred beings, I acquiesce to the term "Masters" for the purposes of honoring both genders of Ascended Human Beings, for indeed they have all clearly mastered themselves.

The eight Ascended Masters who guide me and teach me are: Mother Mary, Lady Quan Yin, Paramahansa Yogananda, Jesus Christ (whom I often call 'Holy Yeshua'), Mary Magdalene, Lord Buddha, Master Lao Tzu, and High Priest Melchizedek.

I am so grateful for their presence in my life, for their love, and for their teachings, which make me whole. This book would neither be possible nor make any sense without them. They are the masters to whom I refer in the title.

Their message to all who read this book is:

We would love to work with you, to guide you to Self-Realization.
With love and devotion, faith and meditation,
you, too, can reach the states of consciousness
necessary to access our spiritual realm
of conscious being.
Allow us to take you on a journey, if you will,
from letting go of your ego-self
to discovering
the full beauty and mastery of your Higher Self,
for this journey will lead you to where
We Are All One.

INTRODUCTION

What does it take to get to where you are able to converse with and be guided by Ascended Masters, and even with God's own self? It depends on where we are on our journey, but at a minimum, in my experience, connection with Ascended Masters and with God requires:

❖   Faith,

❖   Devotion,

❖   A certain degree of purity of intention,

❖   Love for God, Higher Beings, and the spiritual world

❖   Working on one's own inner issues, honestly, openly and with the intent to be transformed into pure Higher Self (and yes, we all have inner issues until we become Self-Realized)

❖   Non-attachment, or loving spiritual reality more than one desires the people, beings, activities, and things of this world. One has to prioritize on a faith journey, and that set of priorities consists of a vastly different list than the priorities of day-to-day life in many of our cultural settings today.

While these priorities can be found in most religions, the mystical experiences common at the mystical level of all religions entail not only these priorities, but also certain spiritual understandings of reality. Indeed, the mystical sense of union is available to all people in all religions and in the absence of religion. Yet, specifically to achieve connection with Higher Beings, it tends to help if one resonates with and lives from the foundation of a few central spiritual concepts.

The spiritual concepts shared in this book represent a synthesis of Eastern and Western spiritual views, based in part on my own intuitive discoveries even before learning to work with the Ascended Masters.

While studying at Vanderbilt University Divinity School, I increasingly began writing intuitively before I even fully understood what that meant. I now understand that writing intuitively means being guided by a connection with a higher consciousness. Intuition comes from our Higher Selves, so whenever I use the word "intuition," I am giving credit to God.

In the fantastic theology program at Vanderbilt Divinity School, I was able to study the "new" physics and process theology together, both of which leave room for free will and randomness in the universe, rather than necessitating or enabling a God who controls. This concept of freedom in the universe along with free will for humans is paramount for the spiritual path. At the quantum level of the universe, there appears to be room both in our understanding and in terms of influence for all kinds of energy and informational processes, including Divine Presence in the forms of consciousness and subtle energy.[1]

In my writings, I was intuitively led to introduce a spiritual paradigm of reality which included God as "an energy presence in creation," thus resonating with ancient Hindu beliefs in the "Aum," or energy emanating from God and creating this dualistic world of Maya. I was not studying such Eastern ideas then, but my intuition led me to an understanding which resonates highly with Eastern monistic thought, which recognizes the duality of Maya, in which Maya refers to the illusory nature of this universe which we refer to as "reality." I was not, at the time, ready for monistic thought, however.

---

[1] What I am referring to here are effects such as the Heisenberg uncertainty principle, the observer effect and quantum entanglement, where physical attributes inspire some physicists to use words such as "mind" and "information," and the possibility exists that our world may be comprised of consciousness which is often measured by physical characteristics. I am fully aware that some physicists object to such metaphysical uses of the quantum lexicon. I still maintain that the "mind stuff" of the universe at the quantum level speaks of who God is. See, for instance, Paul Davies, *The Mind of God: The Scientific Basis for a Rational World*.

Who am I to be writing these things? Well, the most spiritually enlightened answer to that question that I can give you at this time is simply, "Part of the All."

My journey has been long and varied: born on the equator in Africa, and raised in three African countries as well as three different states in the U.S.; widowed at the age of 28 when my 34-year-old husband died of a cerebral aneurysm, leaving me with an infant and a toddler; a single mom for about 16 years; my healing abilities were identified by other people rather than by myself; I learned Raja Yoga meditation in the fall of 1996 and began journeying on an Eastern spiritual path at that time – complete with studies at the Self-Realization Meditation Healing Centre in Somerset, England; I gradually began to develop my intuition, but took a long time to develop faith and trust in God; and eventually, like any good mystic, I fell in love with God.

While I was raised as a Christian, by liberal, intellectual parents, and while I am indeed an ordained minister,[2] my belief system and understanding of reality, including spirituality, has changed enormously over the past eighteen-plus years. Suffice it to say that I shifted very gradually from a strongly Western, rational, scientific mindset, to an intuitive knowing and an Eastern spiritual path full of miracles and wonders, characterized by love, peace, and bliss.

This Eastern path has led me to the point of experiencing direct connection with various Ascended Masters, which connections I will share throughout the book.

What is essential here is that we lay the groundwork for what beliefs can help to enable this kind of journey into the realms of the mystic. We need to delineate what concepts will empower the psyche to be able to explore on different dimensions of reality.

The most basic concept involved here is the idea that we are all on a spiritual journey through life. We are not mere humans living a mortal, material, earthly existence and then we are gone, done, finished with our spiritual work (if we think of ourselves as having any spiritual work to do). Rather, we are souls who came into this lifetime with a purpose, to grow, to learn. We are also here to help create learning opportunities for others – whether we are doing it in a positive sense or in a negative sense. We are here to further our progress as well as the progress of others along a path of life as spiritual beings.

The second most basic concept is that we come here to earth more than once, contrary to the old adage that "you only go around once in life." This adage may have had its roots in rejecting the concept of reincarnation, but it seems to have devolved into meaning "just focus on pleasure, because that's the best we can get in life." To be taught by Ascended Masters, though, it helps to know that we have had many lifetimes, and that we can learn to trust *and* enjoy the journey which will lead us home.

What is our true home? Oneness with the Divine and with all that is of Spirit – that is our true home. In other words, our home is a state of being which may also be called a state of grace. We may experience this state as heavenly, or Nirvana, because it is a state of pure love and peace and bliss.

A fourth helpful spiritual concept is that there are Higher Beings. I choose various terms for the Divine, and I recognize the importance of both genders as expressing aspects of "Who God Is," so I often refer to God as our Divine Mother/Father. In addition, it can be helpful on this mystical journey if we open ourselves to the possibility of encountering angels, archangels, spirit guides, and

16

guardian angels,[3] as well as Ascended Masters.

Ascended Masters, from my understanding of them, are people who walked the earth just as we are doing, but who raised not only their consciousness, but also the vibration of their whole being to an ascended state of being, and who therefore no longer need to be re-born and return to the earth.

Angelic beings refer, in this case, to archangels and angels of light and love who serve Divine Will. If you have trouble believing that they are real, please know that I understand, since I was raised in a home in which we were not allowed to put angels on the Christmas tree, because, as I was told growing up, "angels aren't real." Now, I know they *are* real.[4]

A fifth concept is that we, in our essence, are also Higher Beings. Our True Self is our "Higher Self," which links us directly to God. Our Higher Self also emanates from God as an aspect of God's own Self. Ultimately, our Higher Self returns to Oneness with God someday, after a journey of many lifetimes.

A sixth concept is that what helps us move closer to the Divine on our journey is learning to let go of ego self in order to exist more fully as our Higher Selves. Our Higher Selves are capable of vibrating with unconditional love, compassion, and peace, in ways that our ego selves generally do not even care to do.

A seventh concept is that our egos fulfill essential roles in each lifetime, helping us to develop a sense of self as unique and worth protecting as a physical body. So, our egos keep us alive by working to keep body and soul together. Our egos also help us to develop personalities which enable us and others to learn and grow and enjoy

---

[3] Other terms can be used, such as devas. Also, accessing our ancestors, or souls who have passed on, is often a very real mystical experience for people, and it can be quite helpful and healing.

[4] For a helpful understanding of angels as energies, I highly recommend *Physics of Angels*, by Matthew Fox and Rupert Sheldrake, (San Francisco: HarperSanFrancisco), 1996.

life on our spiritual journeys.

I am sure there are other spiritual concepts that are helpful for experiencing mystical visions, but seven is my favorite sacred number, and these concepts suffice for now to provide a basis for starting to understand the possibilities of mystical journeys in a postmodern world.

It took me a long time to get to this place of feeling comfortable experiencing and openly telling others about my mystical journeys. If all of this seems new to you, please know that I deeply understand and am grateful that you are willing to learn about the possibilities, for your own sake, as well as for understanding and helping others.

I write this book for you, that you may discover your own true inner essence, and that you may re-connect with the fullness of your Higher Self. I pray that you may be able to do so in this lifetime. If you are already aware of your Higher Self, and are seeking to grow on your path, I hope this book will provide you with encouragement to seek to connect and be guided by Ascended Masters.

I pray that you will be filled with and surrounded by the love and light of our Divine Mother/Father as you move forward on your journey, and that you will connect with Higher Beings who will guide you home.

CHAPTER ONE: CHOOSING TO BEGIN
A MYSTICAL PATH

We might want to believe that a mystical path can just happen to us, and in some very real sense, this is so, but truly, we make a choice on some level in order to begin a mystical journey through life.

For me, the mystical journey began in earnest when a friend lent me a copy of the book *Autobiography of a Yogi*, by Paramahansa Yogananda, who founded the Self-Realization Fellowship.

The first time I tried to read *Autobiography of a Yogi*, I literally could not believe the miracles, so I stopped. There are so many miracles in the book, starting even from when Paramahansa-ji[5] was a baby and was able to remember past lives, to be aware of being re-born into this baby's body, and to remember disliking the limitations of a baby's body. The miracles progressed from there, becoming more and more dramatic, and my rational mind just could not believe them. There was, and is, no way to explain such occurrences rationally.

So, I stopped reading it. However, I realized that by not believing the miracles that Paramahansa Yogananda was reporting, I was in essence stating that I did not believe that he was telling the truth. This seemed problematic and extremely disrespectful.

Fortunately, I remembered that I had been raised to practice multi-cultural respect, that is, to appreciate and to respect differing perspectives and values of people who live in different cultures. I realized that I needed to respect that Paramahansa Yogananda was speaking his truth, even somehow the Truth, when he told these miraculous stories. The risk in believing this was that my understanding of reality was going to have to change.

---

[5] Adding "-ji" as a suffix denotes respect, and is customary in recognizing a true guru, or enlightened spiritual teacher.

Well, out of this intention of multi-cultural respect and a desire to learn about his perspective on spirituality, I literally started over, re-reading *Autobiography of a Yogi*. What a difference an open mind and multi-cultural respect can make!

As I read Paramahansa-ji's book, I discovered a whole new sense of reality that had been not only foreign but also unreal to me. Next, I discovered a spirituality that seemed to make sense of life, the universe, and everything in a way that I had been longing for and which no other religious views had been able to do. Finally, I discovered that Paramahansa-ji made sense of Jesus' miracles in a way that no one else had been able to do for me, either: apparently, Jesus was like a Hindu yogi who had mastered himself and developed miraculous powers. Apparently, it is possible to develop such powers, and we are all invited to do so.

Paramahansa Yogananda was also writing during the early days of quantum physics, and he, far better than I, was able to relate the abilities of yogis to the quantum level of reality. My experience with quantum physics has been primarily gleaned from movies such as "What the Bleep Do We Know" and books such as "The Dancing Wu-Li Masters" by Gary Zukav, "A Brief History of Time" by Stephen Hawking, and "The Cosmic Blueprint" by Paul Davies. From reading these perspectives on the universe, as well as from reading *Autobiography of a Yogi,* I have come to the view that, at the quantum level of reality, all is interconnected in such a way that thoughts and their corresponding subtle energies can create change in the observable world of form.[6]

This is, I believe, precisely the understanding of the ancient system of yoga: that our minds project our realities, so that, ultimately, we are co-creators with God, for the mind of God permeates the world

_____

[6] Please understand that I assume full responsibility for my views, and I understand that my views do not necessarily reflect the views of these authors, and in fact may be antithetical to the views of Stephen Hawking. I still greatly appreciate his contributions to science.

as the ever present *Aum*, or creative Word of God which shapes our Universe as well.

From a postmodern perspective, we have deconstructed virtually everything that we could possibly deconstruct, and yet we are also the beneficiaries of quantum views of reality, which paint portraits of an amazing universe, so grand on all its levels. On the one hand then, we have this rational, analytical, often critical and skeptical view of life and the universe, and on the other hand, we have the potential for wonder and awe, unpredictability and grandiosity.

Most importantly, I believe that, in a postmodern reality, we have the freedom to choose our perspectives on life. So it is that I choose the following perspective: we exist in a Universe of "laws" like gravity and thermodynamics, which, though simple and predictable, may be transcended by subtler laws of energy that can only be measured and wielded by the power of consciousness. Consciousness is the most powerful tool we human beings have, second only to the power of love. (I could never describe love as a "tool.")

In fact, I believe that the very reason that double-blind experiments in science have to be "double-blind" is that this is the only way to eliminate the potentially confounding factor of consciousness. One of the teachings I received from the Ascended Masters was, in fact, on the power of consciousness, which may be found in chapter sixteen.

Let's get back to how this slowly acquired understanding of reality, cosmos, and universe came about in my mind. In the fall of 1996, the universe had not only gifted me with the book *Autobiography of a Yogi*, but also, while I was reading it bit-by-bit at night, I was invited to take a week-long, evening class in Raja Yoga Meditation.

The class was taught by a teacher who came over to Michigan from the Self-Realization Meditation Healing Centre in Somerset, England. The story of how I got to take the class is a minor miracle in its own right, given that I was then a single mom and working full-time. At the very least, it was grace embodied through the universe, empowering me to begin a mystical journey.

And yet, it is important to note that I did say "yes," and that I did ask for what was needed in order to take the class. I was not sure why I needed it, except that someone else was recommending it so highly, and I valued and trusted her opinion, and my own intuition must have been resonating with it as well. Saying "yes" to the beginning of our mystical journeys seems to be an important element on our spiritual paths.

So, while reading *Autobiography of a Yogi*, I also got to study Raja Yoga meditation, which is exactly what Paramahansa-ji teaches through the Self-Realization Fellowship of California. Moreover, I got to study with people under a female guru who experienced appearances of Paramahansa Yogananda to her. So, all in all, I was initiated into this mystical reality under the auspices of the line of gurus which included Paramahansa Yogananda.

In this mystical paradigm, nothing truly happens by accident. Believing in freedom and free will in the universe, I would amend that to say that, even whatever happens "accidentally" fulfills spiritual purposes. I believe that there are a range of probabilities for any given point of choice, and that the universe, being a super-computer of sorts, provides beneficial outcomes of one type or another for each potential choice. The beneficial outcomes may not appear beneficial at first, but eventually, the benefit will come.[7]

The benefits for me began from the very first breath and visualization technique that we were taught. In fact, I did not manage to do it correctly the first time I tried it, and because I didn't complete it well, I felt an uncomfortable "buzzing" feeling – a buzzy energy in my whole body. I found out that I just needed to re-finish the visualization technique correctly, and when I did, the buzzing went away.

---

[7] This conceptualization of human freedom and Divine probabilities resonates (to me) with the quantum level in that, when a beam of electrons is sent out, one can predict the pattern that will be formed by the electrons in aggregate, but one cannot predict where any single electron will go.

So, even by doing the first meditative technique "wrong," I was nonetheless introduced to the reality of subtle energy and what it can do on a physiological level. We will talk more about subtle energy in the next chapter.

I was well-taught by the teacher from England. I loved what I was taught, and began to practice it pretty much daily, even though I was a single mom of two school-aged children, and working full-time for a church (which generally means working more than 40 hours a week).

Raja Yoga meditation thus changed my life. As a matter of fact, when combined with the teachings of *Autobiography of a Yogi*, which matched the teachings of the meditation class, the practice of Raja Yoga began to transform my awareness, and eventually my consciousness, first by expanding my ability to sense subtle energies, and then by strengthening my intuition.

During the meditation class, when we were taught a technique which energizes the sixth chakra, or brow chakra, commonly referred to as "The Third Eye," I saw light, and then I saw an eye – a single eye. This signified the opening of my Third Eye. This blossoming of the Brow Chakra essentially expanded my consciousness to be more intuitively aware, and to begin to connect with higher consciousness, although I was quite unaware at the time.

I began to feel some peace when meditating, which was a new experience for me. I generally was living an otherwise stressed-out life as a young widow and single mom. This peacefulness was new, and it was real. I became a fan of Raja Yoga meditation, and actually practiced it whenever I could. Indeed, the meditation class had emphasized the importance of discipline and devotion.

I know I practiced the technique called "sending love." I used it to connect with my mother before she came for a visit, and I believe it increased the sense of harmony between us during her visit. I also "used" the technique of sending love with a man I hoped to draw back into my life, and sure enough, he called me up within 24 hours of my having "sent him love." I began to believe in this subtle energy stuff,

23

and to understand that it was somehow powered by Divine Love.

I began to become a mystic.

CHAPTER TWO: FROM CHAKRAS & SUBTLE ENERGY TO HEALING & MIRACLES

A mystic needs a few good tools for experiencing expanded reality. Meditation is really the best tool that I know. Raja Yoga meditation in particular, along with Kriya Yoga, which is the culmination of Raja Yoga meditation, is designed to raise our energies up the spine in order to develop our chakras, which helps us develop spiritually. Raising energy up our spine and developing our chakras ultimately enables us to progress on our spiritual journeys towards Enlightenment and Self-Realization.

Spiritual disciplines in general help. Spiritual disciplines include, but are not limited to, the following practices:

- ❖ Prayer, which includes prayers of intercession, praying the Rosary, prayers of gratitude, prayers of praise, and so on
- ❖ Meditation – especially Raja Yoga Meditation and Kriya Yoga, but also mantra meditation and other forms as well
- ❖ Devotional reading – reading spiritual or metaphysical books with the intention of growing closer to the Divine
- ❖ Fasting
- ❖ Exercises such as Tai Chi, Qi Gong, Hatha Yoga, and Falun Gong
- ❖ Practicing non-attachment
- ❖ Service – volunteer work, helping, healing, whatever it might be
- ❖ Giving or tithing, and practicing generosity in general
- ❖ Affirmations, breath-work, and visualizations

Prayer in particular can lead to increased intuitive awareness, especially when paired with meditation. However, prayer without the development of the upper chakras, such as that which can result from Raja Yoga meditation, will not necessarily lead to increased intuition.

Prayer, when practiced extensively such as for an hour or more at a time, can lead to a meditative state which can benefit one much like the practice of meditation.

Energy healing also helps. What is energy healing? Energy healing comes in a variety of forms. The most popular or commonly known form of energy healing in America is Reiki,[8] which actually originated in Japan. Energy healing is any modality which operates on the energy system of the body and in which the practitioner herself or himself actually becomes the vessel or channel through which the healing energy flows for the other person.

Energy "work" represents a broader term, for energy work represents any and all modalities which operate on the energy system of the body, which, does not, however, require the practitioner to channel the energy through themselves. Energy work, broadly conceived, can include acupuncture, reflexology, and acupressure, as well as some forms of massage. Massage is not generally taught as an energy modality, but many massage therapists are natural-born healers.

So, what is this energy? Subtle energy or life force is what we are considering here. All living beings have life force energy which keeps them alive. Life force is a form of subtle energy which is available everywhere.

Let's go over subtle energy first. Unless a person is just so shut-off from their own feelings that they cannot feel much of anything, essentially everyone has some awareness of energy. Even those of us who were raised in the rational West, or within the confines of religions which generally choose not to acknowledge such things, we tend to be aware of subtle energy without knowing what it is.

You are probably already an expert in subtle energy but may not know it. Most of us do not have to be taught about subtle energy, because virtually all of us are intuitively aware of it.

---

[8] "Reiki" is a Japanese word which means, in simple terms, "universal life force."

For instance, have you ever been in a room or situation where there was such tension in the air, that you could, metaphorically, "cut the tension in the air with a knife"? Virtually all of us have felt tension in a situation with other people at some point in our lives. And no one had to explain to us that this was tension that we were feeling, because our intuition can detect and understand the message of the subtle energy in the air around us.

Yes, subtle energy has messages to it, such as the subtle energy of "tension in the air." Please think about how common such phrases are. The very commonality of such phrases speaks to the fact that we are all aware of this subtle energy, and that the subtle energy communicates to our intuition what is going on: "people are feeling really tense here!"

Or, for example, have you ever been at a sporting event, perhaps in a big stadium or auditorium, and you could literally "feel the excitement in the air"? Again, please think about how common that language is, because we frequently experience the subtle energy of excitement, and no one has to tell us what that energy is because we intuitively perceive the message of the energy: that a large number of people are feeling really excited all around us.

I could continue on, and usually do in the classes I teach, but I hope you get the idea.

Welcome to awareness of your own expertise in experiencing and identifying subtle energy. You can now become a mystic! Or recognize yourself as already being one!

Our bodies are also systems of energy – organized as a flow of life force. The system of energy in our bodies is organized in patterns of flow to reach the entire body, and part of that system of flowing energy is referred to as the chakra system of the body. Chakra is a word in Sanskrit which means "wheels of light." Chakras can also be described as energy vortices. Our body has seven main chakras organized in relation to the spine, and smaller chakras swirling energy throughout our bodies, including our legs and arms, hands and feet.

The seven main chakras of the body are:

❖ The Base or Root Chakra, located at the base of the spine
❖ The Sacral Chakra, located just below the naval
❖ The Solar Plexus chakra, located just above the naval
❖ The Heart Chakra, located centrally in the chest at the level of the heart
❖ The Throat Chakra, centered in the throat
❖ The Third Eye or Brow Chakra, centered just above and between the eyebrows
❖ The Crown Chakra, or Thousand-Petaled Lotus, located at the top of the head

Each of these chakras serves a particular function in the body, while also affecting our emotional and spiritual well-being, just as it affects our physical well-being. Our subtle energies are really spiritual and emotional energies, which are focused by our thoughts, beliefs, intentions, and feelings. This is part of how our brains affect our bodies: our thoughts, beliefs, intentions and feelings change the subtle energies of our bodies.

As mystics, we need to become more aware of our own energies, whether they are positive and life-giving, whether they are negative, whether they are light and spiritual, or whether they are heavy and very physically and materially-based.

All of the spiritual disciplines, from meditation to energy healing, can help us become more aware of our own energy, and raise our energy vibration to help us advance along the spiritual path.

Energy healing in particular provides a means of cleansing, restoring, and renewing our energies on all levels of our being – physically, emotionally, mentally, spiritually, and energetically. With energy healing, we can:

❖ cleanse the aura

- ❖ balance the chakras
- ❖ feed energy into all levels and all cells of the body
- ❖ calm the mind
- ❖ relax and de-stress the whole mind and body
- ❖ unblock the flow of energy wherever it may be blocked
- ❖ bring healing intentions and energies to increase wellness in specific areas along with general well-being
- ❖ intuitively perceive information according to what is needed

Are "miracles" and mystical experiences possible through energy healing? Of course, very much so. I have experienced dramatic miracles through distance healing, as well as wonderful healings and mystical experiences through energy healing in person.

To invite your belief in such a mystical side of reality, I would like to mention the first three medically or scientifically verified miracles I experienced when giving energy healing, the first of which was for my dog.[9]

At the time, I was living in Kalamazoo, Michigan, with my dog, Comet, and my cat, Picasso. I owned a house in East Lansing, where my daughter lived and paid rent while attending Michigan State University. I paid the balance of the mortgage, in addition to paying rent in Kalamazoo. That meant my budget was pretty tight.

When I moved to Kalamazoo in August of 2007, I discovered the water in the house I was renting was so rusty that it actually ruined some of my clothes. Because my budget was tight, I could not figure out what to do about it, and neither the landlord nor the city would address the issue. (Apparently some municipalities do not define "potable" water sufficiently to protect us and our clothes from rust.) So, I purchased bottled water for myself, and gave tap water to my dog and cat.

---

[9] I was originally told, at age 13, that I could "cure animals with <my> hands," by a gentleman mystic from India who was being studied for his psychic abilities in 1972.

In February of the next year, I was walking Comet on a snowy day and, thanks to the snow on the ground, noticed blood in her urine. When I took her to the veterinarian, they performed an ultrasound of her bladder, and found a mass sticking down like a little, crooked finger.

They recommended that we just give her antibiotics, and see if the blood clears up. I thought at the time, "What are antibiotics going to do for a mass? Nothing, but it's non-invasive, so okay." We put Comet on antibiotics, and the blood in her urine did clear up.

However, ten months later in December of 2008, I was walking Comet and as there was snow on the ground, I was able to see blood in her urine again. I took her back to the vet, and they took another ultrasound, which showed the same little, crooked-finger-shaped mass. The vet said, "We need to do surgery right away, but she's older now, so we'll need to do a liver test to make sure she's healthy enough. Bring her back next week and we'll do a liver ultrasound."

I thought to myself, "If being older is such a concern, why didn't we do the surgery when she was younger? But, okay." We scheduled Comet to return the following Tuesday for her liver ultrasound.

That was on a Friday, I believe. Now, typically, if either Comet or Picasso were sick or hurting, I would feel so emotionally upset that it was difficult for me to give them energy healing, even though I love doing energy healing with animals. However, that next Monday morning, I asked for healing for myself, and during the healing, I heard the intuition, "Now go give healing to Comet."

So, I went downstairs, and asked for healing energy for Comet, and stroked her belly. I mostly had the calm, empty mind which is so essential for the flow of healing energy, but I did have the thought: "I hope they re-do the bladder ultrasound when they do the liver ultrasound."

The very next day, when Comet went to the veterinary clinic, the vet performed the liver ultrasound, and then re-checked the bladder, and the mass was gone. The veterinarian thought she had made a mistake, so she called another vet to do the bladder ultrasound, but the mass which had been there for more than ten months was just gone!

To me, the "moral" of that story is that God loves dogs, too.

ॐ

And yes, of course God loves people.

My first experience of a "minor miracle" with energy healing for a person happened with a friend of mine who smokes, and who developed polyps on her colon. She decided to see me for energy healing before and after her polyp-removal surgery. After the second healing, she returned for her post-operative check-up, and they could not even find any scar tissue!

My second experience of a minor miracle healing with a person involved Dr. Charles Warfield, a beautiful, inspiring soul and stately older gentleman who is one of the pillars of Kalamazoo, especially in church circles as well as in the NAACP, in which he is the president of the local chapter. One day, Dr. Warfield gave a prayer at the end of a clergy meeting, and that prayer helped me. A few months later, at the end of this clergy meeting, he looked as though he was not feeling well, so I offered to return the favor.

It turned out that Dr. Warfield had a kidney stone that was causing him a lot of pain. He allowed me to place my left hand on his left shoulder, and my right hand outside his wool blazer behind the kidney which was hurting. My right hand heated up so much that, through the wool blazer, the heat felt so hot to him that he jumped away saying, "You're going to burn me!"

Dr. Warfield came to see me for several healing sessions, and then went to see his doctor and had an ultrasound of his kidney, which showed the stone was gone, and he had never felt it pass!

God will help us heal ourselves, if we allow God to do so. The mystical presence of God is real, and available to those of us who are willing to pursue this mystical journey, and yes, it is very healing.

ॐ

My original energy healing training was from the centre[10] in England through which I learned the Raja Yoga meditation. I traveled to England for four years in a row to study Progressive Counselling, Natural Spiritual Healing, and Kriya Yoga, as well as to attend Darshan and Satsang with the guru of the centre there. I also took classes taught by teachers from the centre who came over to Michigan, and so I studied animal healing and took meditation refresher classes. Additionally, I took another class entitled something like Energy Management for Health Professionals – in other words, a class on learning how to manage one's own energy for caregivers including physicians, psychologists, healers, nurses, and so on.

To the Self-Realization Meditation Healing Centre I owe a great deal of gratitude for the training I received. I began to have far more powerful experiences of God than ever before in my life while I was there. I am very grateful to everyone there who taught me, and I especially enjoyed the companionship of the other students, who came from several countries around the world. What fun it was!

It was also like spiritual boot-camp. With the international flavor, I often thought of it as the spiritual Olympics. Nonetheless, the final time I was there, I had some experiences which persuaded me that returning there was not something I was likely to need or desire.

Sometimes I do wonder what it would be like to go back, but clearly, I feel the universe has launched me onto a path of leading and creating a new and unique spiritual community here in the United States. The experiences related in this book have led me to a desire to serve God with my whole heart in ways that will reach out with messages of Divine Love and spiritual growth on the path of Self-Realization in new and holistic ways.

My intention is to develop a variety of trainings for people on

---

[10] The Self-Realization Meditation Healing Centre (British spelling), which also spells their Progressive Counselling course according to British English, with two "l's."

the spiritual path, sharing the tools which will help people gain higher consciousness, experience love and peace in life, and even access pure bliss.

Indeed, the Higher Guides invited me, back in December 2012, to begin to teach "Light Worker Training." This story will be shared later; now let's begin the mystical journey. Growing closer to the Divine and being able to work with, talk with, perceive, and simply be with Higher Beings is such a blessing that I invite you to join me in having mystical journeys – a daring choice in this postmodern world.

CHAPTER THREE: BACKGROUND TO THE ENLIGHTENMENT VISION

On Thursday, May 27, 2010, I experienced what I call an "Enlightenment Vision." This vision changed everything for me – it changed life itself; it changed my sense of the universe; it changed the way I "know" things and my connection with the Divine; it changed my being-ness in this universe. To understand how or why this vision occurred to me would be impossible for me to explain in human terms, although it will help if I give some background to it. Please allow me to share some of the experiences that led up to this vision.

Although I began to meditate in 1996, I rarely had significant visionary experiences in the first 13 years of meditating. However, I would like to share my initial experiences of *almost* ascending to a higher realm which I fondly call "the land of foggy white light."

In the years prior to 2010, there were two or three times when I was meditating, that I rose up a column of foggy white light to a circular opening, which was above my head, and around which the Ascended Masters sat in a circle. I felt so honored, these few times that I would get to rise up to just below their feet, even though all I could see was their feet, and maybe the edge of some white robes. Above their feet, the foggy white light blocked my view of them.

This vision was rare, and indeed the visions I experienced only became more frequent after my career as a minister collapsed, and, instead of serving churches, I had a very part-time job, serving a ministerial association. The job was one part administrative assistant, one part clergy volunteer, so the pay was negligible, but the involvement in the community was very rewarding. I was residing in Kalamazoo, Michigan at the time (yes, there really is a "Kalamazoo," and it is a very pleasant community in many ways).

This was the fall of 2009, when I was also writing my first book and volunteering with a faith-based community organizing group, working to expand high-quality early childhood education in Kalamazoo and across Michigan. I was also looking for full-time employment, but this was during the economic downturn, when those of us who were 50 or older particularly found it difficult to find jobs.

During this time, I was invited to attend a spiritual workshop hosted by a large, interfaith group – a lovely group of people, and with a speaker who led us through some spiritual reflection exercises. One of the exercises was to ask our Guides to bring us a gift – at least, that's how I remember it.

The idea of addressing my "Guides" was new to me, and certainly I had never thought to ask for a gift before. I was accustomed to talking with God and with Jesus in prayer, so I asked Jesus for a gift. I then saw Jesus and Mary Magdalene together, and they handed me, from their hands to mine, the gift of a sacred heart.

From my limited knowledge of Catholicism, I was familiar with the concept "the sacred heart of God," and I associated it with both Mother Mary and with Jesus, but beyond that, I did not know the significance of God's sacred heart. Nonetheless, I received the sacred heart as a holy gift, with gratitude, feeling touched by the beauty of Jesus' and Mary Magdalene's holy and loving presence. At that time, I did not pursue further understanding of the gift of the sacred heart, although I cherished the gift.

One other spiritually significant event happened during the fall of 2009, while I was significantly underemployed and writing my first book. I had the opportunity to offer a brief energy healing to a clergy colleague when we attended a clergy gathering. He had significant redness in one eye, so I offered him some healing energy for his eye.

He is a beautiful soul with a real justice orientation to his ministry. However, I knew that he had more of an intellectual and inquisitive faith than a sheer, unquestioning faith in healing energy and divine healing. So, I unwisely prayed, "God, please heal his (name) eye, even if I have to take on his disease myself."

Twenty-four hours later, my right eye started to get red. (I found out much later that his eye got better in about 24 hours.) By the end of the week, the inner corner of my eye looked like red, raw meat. I did an internet search, and discovered that I probably had scleritis, and my eye appeared to be one step from necrotizing scleritis, which can not only make you go blind, but also can kill you.

Although I had no health insurance, clearly I had to go to a doctor, and I did, only to find out that I did indeed have scleritis. The doctor put me on prednisone, something that was way down on my list of things I was willing to do, but I clearly had little or no choice, if I wanted to keep my eye and my life.

Now, the fact is that I was experiencing huge stress at this time, and the gut-wrenching fear I felt about my career and financial situation had a lot to do with my susceptibility to developing this problem.

As a healer, I knew I needed to ask what the inner emotional or spiritual dis-ease was which was causing the outer manifestation of disease. (Even if we can attribute the condition to my prayer during the healing, the way it manifested in me clearly means that I had inner healing to do.) The answer that I received from the Universe via my intuition was not pretty. Clearly I had work to do on myself.

From then on, the scleritis became for me a spiritual barometer of how I was doing; whether I was having faith and trusting God, and loving others equally as myself, or not. It also clearly reacted both to eating too much sugar and to drinking wine. I was already a vegetarian, but the red eye became an invitation to reduce both my sugar intake and to stop having that occasional glass of red wine.

More spiritual lessons in non-attachment! For a while, though, I let myself be talked into eating just meat and vegetables to reduce the inflammation, but the energy of eating meat was just too heavy for me; I could only do it for a month or two, and then stopped.

The energy of eating meat just does not match the very light and pure energy I experience and feel I need when doing energy healing, nor even the lightening of energy I feel while meditating.

In January 2010, I was meditating more and starting to experience more visions and more thoughts, or voice messages, in my head. Sometimes I felt as though I were going crazy. Fortunately, I was reading Caroline Myss's *Anatomy of the Spirit,* in which she writes about such challenges associated with becoming a mystic.[11] How nice to know that I was not alone in feeling as if I were going crazy! Also, while reading Myss's book, I realized for the first time that I was becoming a mystic. That made sense!

I was also reading the delightful book, *The Physics of Angels,* by Matthew Fox and Rupert Sheldrake. The book itself delighted me for its combination of science, spirituality, and sacred history of – yes, mystics. In this book, I learned the concept that angels are energies from God. This is a very helpful perspective for energy healing.

During this period of increasing mystical experiences, I talked with Jesus, and felt him withdrawing from me. He told me that I needed to learn to "work directly with the angels" myself. I was not sure what that meant, but I realized that he meant I could not just depend on other Spiritual Masters, but rather, I had to become one myself.

That was the spiritual side of my life, and it was only barely supported by the combination of my part-time work with rare energy healing work. I call this time in my life my "Buddhist begging bowl" phase, in which I was occasionally supported by my father, and quite regularly by a beautiful retired soul who graciously helped me to pay rent time and again. I am so grateful for these two men, who literally enabled me to keep a roof over my head, and food on the table. I am also grateful for my landlord, who was very supportive and understanding through this time period.

Since my career had taken a nose-dive, and since the average time for a minister to find a new job was several months, I was looking

---

[11] Caroline Myss, *Anatomy of the Spirit: The Seven Stages of Power and Healing,* (New York: Three Rivers Press), 1996.

at possibly a long time before finding another ministerial position. Church politics was my weak point, although I loved preaching, teaching, and pastoral care. One has to be good at the politics to survive as a minister, as well as to find a new job.

So, in an attempt to provide for myself, I had signed up with one of these businesses that charge way more than an arm-and-a-leg to help you build a website (one of the most ignorant and worst decisions of my life), and then I had also paid inordinately too much to another business for assistance forming a corporation and handling taxes (possibly the other worst decision of my life), so I was massively in debt, and trying to build a website to sell things which I had never sold before. I was not doing well at that. As a matter of fact, while I learned a lot about internet sales, and health-related products that I wanted to sell, I had sold nothing at all.

I was also writing my first book, *Aging Well ~ Be Your Best Self Forever*. I had felt deeply moved to write this book when Michael Jackson died, because we were the same age, and I was surprisingly young-looking and healthy at that time, despite the opposite nature of my finances and career compared to Michael Jackson's fabulous success. Because of the contrast in his health and wealth to mine, I felt inspired to write about what enabled me to be so healthy and happy, without all that fame and fortune. The book just bubbled out of me.

Even though I loved writing the book and my part-time job was pleasant, I was earning very little money at the time. I would occasionally get to do an energy healing for someone, but I really only had had two repeat clients, plus a couple of neighbors who appreciated my healing work with people or with their pets, although that was more of a trade, because we had a small circle of wonderfully supportive neighbors at our end of the street.

Even though this time period was tough in my life financially, I would like to point out that God did provide for me. Not only did God provide for me, often through other human beings, but God also enabled me to keep a promise I had made to care for the orphans of a Congolese woman who had died of HIV. Having returned to the Congo in 2005, my daughter and I had started selling fair trade items to help out people in Kinshasa. This fair trade project had led to supporting three orphans, who did suffer a shortage of food from how little I was able to send, but who have survived and attended school all these years. I am especially grateful to those who have helped me keep my promise when I needed help doing so.

One week in May of 2010, my financial situation hit rock-bottom. I had been significantly underemployed for almost a year. There was practically no money in the bank, my savings were gone, and I had already been helped so many times by others that I couldn't easily ask for more. Life was looking harder than ever. Again, I was faced with the question, "how am I going to pay the rent?"

That Monday, I also received in the mail a letter from the IRS stating that I owed penalty taxes on the corporation I started the year before to sell health products on a website that never sold anything, because I didn't know the filing deadline for corporations was before the filing deadline for individuals, and I filed late. I knew I did not have that money on hand, let alone the rent. I did not yet know if I was going to have even a part-time job during the summer; I had no predictable, visible income in sight.

That Monday evening, though, I had a healing scheduled with my one repeat client that year. She's a lovely young woman who was at the time a resident physician, about to go off and become an attending somewhere. For the first time, I shared with her a little about my situation.

She said to me, "You're such a gifted healer! You need to stop being so timid and put yourself out there. You should contact yoga centers in Saugatuck and South Haven and see if you can teach meditation there in the summer when they have tourists!"

What a needed affirmation! So many of the people I knew at that time, including friends, simply did not believe there is any benefit to energy healing, in general – nothing to do with my work in particular. As a matter of fact, most of the people I knew at that time in my life did not understand the benefits of energy healing. So, I had spent most of my time speaking to deaf ears, feeling so unnecessary in the lives of others, while knowing that my gifts had been buried. Essentially, it meant the universe was mirroring back to me my own lack of faith in myself as a healer, a minister, and a servant of God.

What a painful place that had been in which to live. Of course, I now know that the lack of faith I had in myself at that time originated in myself. But all the while, I had also known the truth of my healing client's words: "You're such a gifted healer!" I am so grateful that she spoke those words out loud, and to me, for it is the recognition of the gift of God which is within me, not the recognition of myself, but of God through me.

Then, when I shared with my healing client that I had started this website, but that I really felt that God did not want me to be doing it, but it was kind of late now, because I had already started it, she simply said, "If you think that God doesn't want you doing it, then why are you doing it?"

That was helpful. Very direct, and very helpful. Sometimes the right question is all we need to hear.

So, I decided that I would stop doing the website. The next day, which was Tuesday, I called the merchant processing solutions through my bank, and they told me that it would cost $295 in early termination fees, but to go ahead and send a fax.

Oh, dear, $295 on top of whatever the IRS wants and I had no idea where to find that money, let alone to pay the rent. And I really wanted to find a way to afford to get down to Texas for my parents' sixtieth wedding anniversary and my niece's wedding in June. How was any of this going to happen? Especially since I still did not know if I was going to be working even part-time during the summer.

This challenge looked worse than anything I had ever experienced in my life. It looked so awful, I decided it was amazing. And once I decided that this was an amazing challenge, I decided I just had to enjoy it. There was nothing else to do! This challenge was simply *so* amazing, why not marvel at it and tackle it with relish? So I did.

No doubt it helped a lot that my daily devotional reading at this point was a combination of re-reading *Autobiography of a Yogi*, and reading Matthew Fox's *The Coming of the Cosmic Christ*. Paramahansaji's book can help instill faith like no other book I've read (except, perhaps, the Bible), and Fox's book helped me understand the mystical journey intellectually, historically, and cosmically.

One morning of that incredibly challenging week, as I meditated, I was taught the true nature of what it means to be a spiritual warrior. Now, despite having read Dan Millman's *A Peaceful Warrior* long before, as a feminist raised in a long-line of pacifists, I considered the term "spiritual warrior" quite unappealing. In fact, I had stayed away from the term 'spiritual warrior' because I perceived it as being a male-dominant way of being in the world, and not usually a peaceful one at that. But God sometimes has interesting ways of getting points across in our heads, and what I learned was beautiful.

What came to me is that warriors serve a higher entity, not themselves, and they stand against something or someone until they themselves can no longer stand, or until that something or someone runs away or falls down before them. A spiritual warrior does not necessarily fight, and certainly does not necessarily kill, but a spiritual warrior does stand up, and stand long, and stand strong in the face of the 'enemy' or the challenge, or the quest on which they are sent by that higher power.

Another teaching that came to me while I was meditating is that a warrior metaphorically represents the opposite of a victim. The victim is the one who falls down, and who on some level of their being gives up or allows themselves to be defeated. I suppose a coward runs away, and then may hide, so cowards are neither victims nor warriors,

41

just cowards, who, by their own fearful actions, may victimize themselves. But warriors stand there as long as humanly possible, or longer, with divine help, until that which they oppose gives up, or can neither overcome nor get around the warrior's strength.

God was inviting me to look at the challenges of my life as a spiritual warrior: to see myself serving a higher power (God/Love), and to stand in service to Love no matter what challenges I face, rather than lamenting them, complaining about them, or wishing I could run away from them.

And certainly, a spiritual warrior is never abandoned by the one he or she serves (at least not if we are serving Divine Love and Truth and Light). So, when we face the challenges of life in service to Divine Love, this Love never abandons us, but serves instead to make us stronger in the face of the challenges which we seek to defeat or overcome.

Choosing to be a spiritual warrior means giving up the victim mentality, and rather than giving up, it means continuing the quest to serve, standing for some higher purpose and for Someone higher, even when we appear to be losing or things appear not to be going our way. A spiritual warrior never stops standing for God, for truth, for justice, for Love, no matter what the challenges may be.

This is a peaceful way of being, because it stands for something, as well as standing against something, which could be injustice or failure or dishonesty, or any number of life-denying intentions. A spiritual warrior continually works on acquiring the inner strength to keep standing, inner wisdom to know how to stand and what to stand against, as well as inner discernment to recognize those people and events in life that are standing for the higher power, as well as those that are standing against the higher power.

What the spiritual warrior fights is his or her own desire to give up, give in, or otherwise succumb to defeat. Spiritual defeat is not an option when serving Divine Love. Love wins. Spiritual warriors who stand on the side of love win the war, even if they must lose a few battles in the process of being on the winning side.

42

Such a spiritual warrior can be male or female, even though this kind of strength is generally seen as a masculine kind of strength, and the warrior image tends to be seen as a masculine image. Spiritual warriors have both masculine and feminine strengths: they are incredibly strong inside themselves, and yet gentle with both self and others as much as possible. Spiritual warriors are men and women who serve the Divine, stand in the strength of Divine love and Divine Truth, and stand for that truth and love to benefit others, everywhere, always, and as long as possible.

With that lesson, I made the incredibly important shift away from being a victim, to being a spiritual warrior. I can tell you that, widowed at the age of 28, with significant knee problems, probable Attention Deficit Disorder and a host of other challenges, along with about sixteen years as a single mom, I had become a specialist at victim consciousness!

During meditation after I made this essential shift, I had a vision in which I got to rise up to stand in the land of foggy white light – the place where one could meet the Ascended Masters. And there, I saw Paramahansa Yogananda himself grinning at me! Paramahansa-ji threw his arms around me and gave me a big hug!

This was really a hugely significant gift to me, for several reasons. First, of course, I was being hugged by Paramahansa Yogananda – an Ascended Master, guru, and yogi, in person, as it were!

Secondly, I had long wondered whether or not Paramahansa Yogananda would accept me, since folks at the spiritual centre where I studied seemed to me (I could be mistaken – but this was definitely how I experienced them) to consider my feminist values to be coming fom ego, particularly my passion for gender-inclusive language[12]. And of course, writing in India and America of the early twentieth century, Paramahansa Yogananda generally used gender-exclusive language for people, as was the custom in English, despite his devotion to the Divine Mother which he expresses so beautifully.

Third, this vision was significant because I had been re-reading *Autobiography of a Yogi*, and was feeling guided by Paramahansa to invite others to learn about and to experience the path to Self-Realization.

Well, and of course, the vision was huge because Paramahansa-ji smiled at me and hugged me! I could never have dreamed of that happening on my own – it had to be a legitimate reality that came to me, unbidden, though perfectly welcome.

Lastly, the vision seemed especially significant in that I got to stand on the same plane with the Ascended Masters. Wow! What an honor, not in an ego sense, just in the sense of recognition of the reality of the journey of my soul. That feels absolutely humbling, by the way, because one realizes that one has not gained worthiness, but that one has been made worthy, by emptying oneself.

Well, the next day, Wednesday, I found out that I would be able to work part-time during the summer. I also went to my bank, to send the fax to cancel the merchant services, and there the business account manager told me she could cancel the termination fees once they hit my account!

I hadn't yet called the IRS, but I trusted that God and I would somehow manage that one also, hopefully with a gracious payment plan agreement with the IRS. How funny that things just began to smooth out!

---

[12] Gender inclusive language refers to using expressions such as "humankind" rather than "mankind" and "family" or "siblings" rather than "brotherhood," and "community" rather than "fellowship." The reason for such language is to honor the sacred feminine as equal with the sacred masculine, to affirm the sacred feminine within us all, and to affirm and empower women and girls, hopefully overcoming the lingering sexism, rape, abuse and even prevalent androcentrism still present in most cultures and religions in the early 21st Century.

Actually, in many ways, when I was not feeling the anxiety over my financial situation, I found that focusing on my spiritual life rather than on a job and career felt incredibly freeing. When one is focused on the spiritual level of reality instead of the physical, material, and financial aspects of reality, one becomes set free in a way that no words can describe. A spiritual focus in life also leads one to a much deeper understanding of what is truly important in life. I am grateful for the times I have been set free from the cycle of work, earn money, pay bills, work...etc. Life is surely much more than this!

For a few weeks prior to this week, there had been numerous times of absurdity (mostly challenging difficulties) in my life, and at those times, I had felt and heard someone inside me, laughing. Again, I heard, sensed, and felt, the joy and release of an inner laughter.

And then, on Thursday, I sat to meditate for a second time in the middle of the day – one of the best luxuries of working only part-time. I was transported in a vision more remarkable than any I had ever had before. This vision took all the visions I had ever had, and even added altogether, surpassed them entirely.

CHAPTER FOUR: ENLIGHTENMENT VISION

On Thursday, May 27, 2010, I received the gift of the most blessed vision I have ever received. As I took time for a mid-day meditation, I had a vision in which I once again got to rise into the "Land of Foggy White Light" to stand with the Ascended Masters. At first, I could not see them. So, I prayed, "Please let me see the truth of your being. Please also let me see the truth of your being with me."

I don't rightly know how the words for that particular prayer came to me; those were just the words I needed most at that time, and so they came to me, as what we most truly need always comes to us when we are in line with the divine will.

In the vision, immediately after I prayed, a man with an Asian appearance greeted me with the folded hands and bowed head of 'Namaste.' He looked like a holy monk. As I tried to bow to his feet, first signaling recognition of an Enlightened One by raising my hands above my head in prayer position, then to my forehead, then to my heart in Namaste, he shook his head at me, as if saying that I was just to return the greeting of Namaste, as if recognizing me as an equal.

There was a pause, while I humbly soaked in this recognition of equality with an overwhelmed and grateful heart.

Next, Mother Mary appeared to me. I had prayed to her many times to ask her for assistance when I do healing work, as well as often times before my meditations. Mother Mary gave me a rose, and said to me, "A sign of the sacred feminine within you."

Then, Mary Magdalene greeted me, and I asked if we could be sisters. (I have no idea why this particular prayer was my request, but again, it must have been the one that was needed.) Mary Magdalene answered, "Yes, as long as you will let me live inside you." In other words, I am to make space for her divine presence by being emptied of myself.

Jesus appeared, although I could not really tell you what he "looked" like. He took this idea of emptying myself further. When I realized that Jesus was with me, tears began to stream down my cheeks on my physical body, not in the vision. At that moment that I felt the tears, I temporarily felt my body below me, as it were, while I was in this ascended state/place. And then my awareness was back "up."

Jesus placed a mantle on my shoulders – I could feel its weight; it was made of off-white cotton or linen, but with a substance to it, representing responsibility for others. Having worn clergy stoles for years, I experienced this mantle as a sacred stole, except that it was twice as wide, and twice as heavy as a regular clergy stole. Perhaps the significance is twice the responsibility and perhaps twice the authority. At any rate, it was big and heavy!

I told Jesus that I would like to follow him, and he pointed up into the blue sky, and told me that I needed to be willing to become a little point in the blue. I told him that I understood his point (a pun Jesus and I made together!) In other words, I must dissolve myself into the greatness of God.

Paramahansa Yogananda told me he would work with me. I am particularly grateful for this promise, because I need his help in bringing through the concept of Self-Realization in this culture, and in this time.

Buddha laughed and revealed that it had been he who had been laughing inside my head to get me to laugh at myself. Buddha told me to keep laughing at myself.

I asked to see and to give thanks to the Reiki Masters, which did not make that much sense, since I had already seen Mother Mary, Jesus, and Buddha, each of whom I had been taught were Reiki Masters. Yet, when I asked to see the Reiki Masters, an Asian man, perhaps Master Usui, who was responsible for bringing the practice of Reiki to the world, appeared and bowed in Namaste to me. I could not see the seven Reiki Masters all at once, though I had already seen three of them.

I also asked to see the angels and archangels who help me with healing. Archangel Raphael in particular had been helping me with healing, but also, I had learned to ask Archangel Michael for help and

48

protection as well. I did not directly see angels, but I saw and sensed pure light, which was precious beyond words to convey. It was though I was seeing rainbow flashes of light, like prisms, dancing within the white light.

I was told, "Welcome to the Seven Rays." Although I knew that there are Seven Masters and Seven Rays of light in Reiki, I really had no idea what this statement meant. So, I asked, "What does that mean?"

The answer I heard was: "You have become someone who is capable of holding all Seven Rays, and of being a channel of the rays for others."

I was in such awe, I was speechless.

An elegant Asian lady, whom I believe to be Lady Kwan Yin,[13] came to me and with her own thumb, anointed or marked my Third Eye with a red dot or oval. Thank you, Sacred Lady. Lady Kwan Yin is one of the Reiki Masters.

I asked to see High Priest Melchizedek, because he is one of the Reiki Masters, and also because, according to the Bible, Jesus is ordained in the priesthood of Melchizedek. I had been told by another clergywoman that Catholic priests are ordained into this priesthood, and maybe Episcopalians as well, but not other Protestant clergy.

High Priest Melchizedek appeared, looking very kingly. I asked why he was dressed like a king, and he replied, "so that you would recognize me." I asked him if my ordination was in his line, and he replied, "No, but it can be." He then poured oil over my head, to make me "An Anointed One." I was so grateful, I tried to hug his feet, but I was told not to do that, for the divine presence is in me as well. Tears of joy streamed down my face.

I realized that ordination in the line of Melchizedek represents far more than what ordination has been reduced to in both the

---

[13] Or Quan Yin. The spelling of her name in English varies with translation from either her Chinese name or the Japanese variation of her name.

49

Protestant and the Catholic traditions, as well as in Christianity in general. The Ordination I received from High Priest Melchizedek was to become an Anointed One, that is, a Christ Presence on Earth. This is a similar concept to Self-Realization and God-Realization in Hindu thought, or becoming Awakened and a manifestation of Buddha himself in Buddhism. Or, at the very least, it is an awakening of the Christ-Consciousness within oneself.

Tears of joy and adulation were streaming down my face as I came back into my body. Then, I got to leave it briefly to go back up to be part of the blue sky, looking down upon the earth, as part of the circle of angels who hold divine loving and healing energy for the earth around the equator.

This was the second time I had experienced this out-of-body circle with the angels. Both times, I was above the equator over South America, which seems unexpected, since I was born on the equator in Africa. As I encircled the earth with the angels, I was suddenly filled with an overwhelming Love for all life – all people, all living beings, even ants, and for Mother Earth herself. All of a sudden, I understood that being filled with this overwhelming Love is apparently the same as being part of the Sacred Heart of God.

As soon as I understood the truth of the Sacred Heart of God, whoosh! I was back in my body on earth. The vision had ended.

O Divine Love, I thank you, I praise you; I seek you with all that I am! To our Divine Father/Mother be the praise and the glory for this vision. Aum and Amen.

CHAPTER FIVE: THE THRESHOLD OF CHRIST-CONSCIOUSNESS

For a few days after the Enlightenment Vision I had on May 27, 2010, I felt a sense of peace, deepened faith, and great joy. I felt as though I knew that God was actually part of every moment of my life, and that everything would be okay, even when it didn't feel easy, or fun, or even 'safe.'

Buddha still laughed within me, and I found that laugh so reassuring!

I think I'm learning what it means to 'work directly with the angels,' as Jesus told me to do. As the book *The Physics of Angels* explains so well, one way of understanding angels is as energies that emanate from the Divine. This understanding only makes sense if we remember that subtle energies carry messages with them, as we learned in chapter two. So then, angels carry Divine energy and Divine messages into the universe, wherever they are needed.

For about 24 hours, I just let the vision sink in. That same evening, I had attended a meeting at which I was a volunteer, and I was in such a profound state of peace that I found it hard to speak. So, I just let the peace stay with me for a while.

Part of me wondered if I was having delusions of grandeur, and felt very concerned about that. In addition to the numerous people who liked and loved and appreciated me, I knew a number of people who did not see me as an especially good or loving person. Of course, we can only see people as we are, so if we are judgmental, we will more likely experience others as judgmental, and if we are loving, we will more easily experience others as loving, and so on. Who we are is rarely perceived in any "pure" sense by others, because our view of others is so limited, or expanded, by who we are ourselves.

In other words, our ability to understand and to perceive others as they are is limited by where we are in our level of spiritual development, or by our progress on the spiritual path. So, I was thankful (and am still thankful) that there were people who loved and

51

understood and appreciated me.

Then it dawned on me that perhaps, since the Enlightenment Vision was so big, it was definitely not about me, but about far more than just me. That made perfect sense, so I started to do an internet search about the astrological significance of the day.

I found a website that affirmed the day as "The Blessing of the Christ Fest," and as a time when the "World Teacher" brings forth higher wisdom for the earth. It also happened to be the third full moon of spring, and the moon was in Sagittarius, which is my sign.[14] This site also affirms that the second full moon of spring is the Wesak Festival, celebrating the "Eternal Buddha Nature," which is what the World Teacher then brings forth with the third full moon, or Christ Fest.

So, not only do we have an affirmation of Buddha's teaching within me, it seems that indeed, the vision was about bringing through higher wisdom, or Christ-consciousness. I receive that mantle with utmost humility and enthusiastic gratitude.

For four days after the vision, I lived in peace and solitude with the beauty of the vision before I shared the vision with anyone. (This fact alone was so unlike the ego-self in me that always shared the drama of my life as soon as possible!) Then I shared it with two women friends who came over for Memorial Day. I was so grateful for the vision that I needed to celebrate and give thanks for it, and it helped to share the celebration with friends who did not tell me that I was delusional! What wonderful friends they are indeed!

I began to journey through life post-Enlightenment Vision. My sense of self as well as purpose and perspective changed greatly, though my life did not immediately change. I sensed an ongoing connection with the Divine and with Higher Beings that was greater than anything I had ever experienced before.

---

[14] I am gratefully indebted to Robert Wilkinson and his site: www.aquariuspapers.com

Indeed, on an on-going basis, I began to hear what I thought of at the time as "The Teacher Voice." Perhaps this name echoed the concept of "The World Teacher" coming through into our consciousness in this world on that third full moon – the Christ Fest. Perhaps the Teacher Voice was the voice of an Enlightened One (an Ascended Master), or of an angel or archangel. At any rate, the voice in my head certainly sounded like a teacher from a higher realm, whose consciousness and awareness were highly elevated compared to our normal ego-states of consciousness.

Nonetheless, having a vision such as I had is not an easy thing to live with in the sense of maintaining that higher consciousness; one does not just wake up a completely different person the next day. I still had the same 51-year-old body with all its challenges, and the same desire to stay up late and sleep in, and so on. The difference was the energy of peace and love and the higher consciousness of which I was more fully aware than ever before.

Living on a day-to-day basis, I would go in-and-out of a sense of connection with the Divine. As I began to struggle with a sense of disconnection with the Presence of the Divine within me, I kept hearing the Teacher Voice in my head saying, "Pranayamas, pranayamas! You need pranayamas."

I knew from reading *Autobiography of a Yogi* that pranayamas are certain types of breath-work that increase one's prana, or life force. At a minimum, they increase the life force in the body as we breathe in. Ultimately, pranayama breathing can help one attain enlightenment, accomplish miracles, or perform other amazing feats, like slowing your heart rate and breathing significantly.

However, I clearly didn't have a sense of what they are, how to do them, or what they would do. I kept feeling guided to be aware of breathing in prana a certain way each time I breathe, whenever I needed to connect. When I did so, it felt as though my body became less substantial and more ethereal.

I was also guided to see every breath as a temple of Divine Presence, for every breath brings us the gift of Life. Every breath thus becomes an opportunity to be grateful, to worship, to devote ourselves to Divine Presence. By breathing consciously as though every breath is a temple, we can also raise our consciousness at any time (so long as we're still breathing!).

Since I was being told by the Teacher Voice that I needed pranayamas, I tried checking online for pranayamas, but did not feel content with the results of my first search. Perhaps listening to the angels is meant to be more of a direct connection than an internet/cyber connection! Actually, in the years since then, I have often found confirmation online of what I have been taught through mystical or intuitive experiences – so the learning has often happened directly from higher sources into my consciousness, and the internet has been helpful for confirmation and further explanation a number of times.

As a wonderful follow-through by the "Higher Ups," as I now fondly call the Ascended Masters, angels, and Archangels who bless and guide me, I did learn some pranayama breathing from two different sources within a couple of weeks.

The first follow-through happened as I took my healing client's advice, and reached out to Satya Yoga, a studio in Saugatuck, Michigan, along Lake Michigan, one of Michigan's vacation spots for people from Chicago, and around the world. Michele Adrianse, the founder and former owner of the studio is delightful and gracious. Michele happened to teach me the very form of pranayama that I needed to help keep my crown chakra open, although I did not really and truly realize that this was what I was needing to do, or that I was opening my crown chakra when I did that.

I received a "direct" teaching to go along with this pranayama as well. I was intuitively given a phrase to affirm after doing the breathing exercise a few times. Later, I was re-reading part of Paramahansa Yogananda's *Autobiography of a Yogi* and discovered that the phrase made perfect sense for opening the crown chakra.

Also, Michele directed me to a yoga studio called "Power of Breath" in Portage, Michigan, a small suburb of the already small city

54

of Kalamazoo, Michigan. At this yoga practice, I learned a series of breathing and stretching techniques, some of which I still practice because they are so perfect for de-stressing, releasing anxiety, and getting centered in Divine Love.

In fact, the stretching and breathing routine that I learned there is so helpful that I teach it, with a few minor variations, to my clients as well as to our new spiritual community.[15] So, I give credit to Power of Breath Yoga for their lovely teachings, and am so grateful to them as well as to Satya Yoga, for bringing me what I needed to raise, or keep raised, my consciousness from ego-consciousness to crown-chakra consciousness.

It was also at Power of Breath that I experienced, for the first time, praying to be centered in Higher Consciousness and then being accompanied by the higher energies that I associate with the Ascended Masters and Archangels. I felt this Presence with and through me was confirmed by the elderly mother of the teachers at Power of Breath, who honored me by her response to my greeting, and who told me she felt we had been together in a previous lifetime. I am sure it was the energy of the Higher Beings that were with me that connected with her own Higher Self energy in recognition. What an honor!

In the meantime, though, within a week of the Enlightenment Vision, I had started to feel as though I was not fully maintaining that connection with Presence (or Higher Consciousness), primarily due to the bad habit of neglecting to ask to be guided in every moment of every day and of not always heeding the guidance I did receive.

So, Thursday one week after the vision, I prayed to be shown how to work with the angels directly. Then I met a friend at lunch, and she was the third person with whom I shared the vision. She was very excited for me and with me about the vision. I told her I was concerned that people would not understand the significance of it, and

---

[15] In September 2014, a few friends and I started the Self-Realization Community. Please see: http://selfrealizationcommunity.org/

that it seems to be about enlightenment and attaining Christ-Consciousness. I believe she understood and accepted this significance. I cannot tell you how reassuring it was to have some friends respect this experience, because I was still so full of doubt about myself.

Later that same afternoon of the day I had prayed to learn to be guided by the angels, the angels started teaching me. Since I felt that I had not done well at maintaining Christ-Consciousness since the vision, first they taught me the relationship between Enlightenment and Christ-Consciousness.

Please understand that I have come to an awareness that Christ-Consciousness and Buddha-Consciousness are essentially the same level of awareness, or extremely similar ways of being, and that one may use similar terms such as Enlightened Consciousness or Unity Consciousness.

I will often use the term Christ-Consciousness, though, in part because Paramahansa Yogananda[16] uses the term as well, and also because I was raised and trained in the Christian tradition, and at the time in my life when I had the Enlightenment Vision, the Christian faith was still primary for me.

What I learned from the angels was as follows:

Enlightenment is the threshold through which one passes in order to attain Christ-Consciousness. Enlightenment is the threshold to the *realm* of Christ-Consciousness (or Buddha-Consciousness). When one passes through the doorway of Enlightenment, one is Awakened to this higher state of consciousness.

Enlightenment is an awakening, while Christ-Consciousness is a way of knowing, out of which arises a way of living and doing. This is why Jesus said, "I am the way…" The Christ Presence Within is the way to God. Having Christ-Consciousness means being on a continual

---

[16] Founder of the Self-Realization Fellowship and author of many books, including *Autobiography of a Yogi*. Paramahansaji is also one of my beloved Guides.

path to God, in the sense of already being there, even while we're on the way. It's "both-and," in the sense that we know our unity with the Divine, and yet live on this earth plane with awareness of lower consciousness as well as the Higher Consciousness, yet the Oneness prevails. In order to maintain Christ-Consciousness as a permanent state of being, I was told that one has to pass four tests. I did not immediately find out what those tests were, however.

Now, it just so happened that, as I was walking with my dog the next morning, I stated to God that I wanted to be of service to others, putting others before service to myself. This means serving what is in their highest good, not serving their ego selves. When I made that declaration, I was told that I had just passed the first test.

"How many tests are there?" I asked. "Four," I was told. Gradually, the four tests were revealed to me, slowly enough to give me time to absorb the meaning of each one.

The Four Tests for Attaining and Maintaining Christ-Consciousness:

(1) Hold the pure intention of service to others before service to self. This service is intended for the highest good of all, rather than service to the ego self.

(2) Let go of all that is not God; hold continually onto love alone.

(3) Refuse to idolize one's self or even one's Self. This idolization derails some enlightened ones as we all find ourselves strongly tempted to focus on our own attainments. We must worship our Divine Source alone. We must appreciate and love all life which emanates from God, but we must worship God alone.

(4) Life is a game of illusion; the hard work of compassion alone evens the score.

I was not clear about the meaning of this fourth test when it first came to me, but I believe it has become clear to me now. All I understood at the time that I received this message was that compassion is the emphasis of the Christ-Conscious life. Also, bringing compassion into the world can be hard work even to focus on within oneself, especially since so many of us are bound up by the illusions of the ego and of the material world.

So many of us human beings are caught up in the illusion that one has to "win" in life, whether winning means career success, being healthy, earning a lot of money, getting what we want, or doing what we want, and so on.

If Maya as illusion reduces life to a game, where some are "winners" and some are "losers," I believe the only true way to 'win' is to live a life of compassion. Fortunately, compassion makes other people winners; hence, it evens the score for others, rather than for ourselves. Perhaps part of the illusion of Maya is that we are to win, when in fact, at the level of Christ-Consciousness or Buddha-Consciousness, the purpose is to ensure that other people win.

Perhaps compassion is the very means by which we can escape the illusion of life, or Maya, itself. That is, living a life completely dedicated to service and compassion can break the cycle of re-birth into this world of Maya. Thus, compassion is the only way for us to "win," as well, in the sense of ultimate Divine Union, but we can only win by ensuring that others win!

I believe that, when Jesus said, "the last shall be first and the first shall be last," this is part of what he meant. Out of compassion, we put others first. Whether or not we ever come first really does not matter, for in the end, in the compassionate heart of God, we all win.

CHAPTER SIX: THE LESSONS CONTINUE

Life began to shift in some positive directions, perhaps with baby steps, and in the meantime, the lessons I received from the Ascended Masters continued. Small graces occurred on the physical plane, such as finding out that my part-time job would continue during the summer – what a relief!

In the meantime, my intuitive learning grew by leaps and bounds. It was as though having my crown chakra open up enabled a direct communication with God on an on-going basis. The truly funny part of all this was the degree to which I kept doubting myself, so that, even as I learned about ways to maintain higher consciousness, I still doubted myself as being capable of having higher consciousness – let alone an open crown chakra!

The real and perfect test for this higher consciousness presented itself: the opportunity to spend time with most of my family!

As I mentioned earlier, my parents' sixtieth wedding anniversary was scheduled to be celebrated on June 10th, followed by my niece's wedding, both occurring in or near San Antonio, Texas. My father generously sent me $2,000 so that I could get the tires on my car replaced, pay some bills, and afford to drive down there. I don't remember which bills I was able to pay; perhaps it was the IRS. This was truly welcome help, though obviously a temporary solution to my financial situation. I am so grateful to my father for his generosity.

As life and timing would have it, it was just the day before I was to leave for San Antonio that I got to drive to the yoga center in Saugatuck and learned what seemed to be the perfect pranayama for keeping one's crown chakra open.

I drove to Saugatuck, met Michele, had a lovely visit, learned the pranayama, explored the possibility of doing workshops or energy healing in Saugatuck, and then drove home that evening. This means that I had to pack, do laundry, and prepare for the trip late that night, as well as the next day, including preparing for my dog and cat to be left in the care of neighbors.

As a result, I began my over 1,300-mile trip from Kalamazoo, Michigan, to San Antonio, Texas about halfway through the day. I already felt exhausted from staying up late, so as I drove, I realized I had the challenge of staying awake while driving long-distance alone.

To increase my energy, I began using my newly-learned pranayama, which not only helped me stay centered but also made me feel more alert and energized. I was able to drive the entire distance without taking a nap, although clearly I had to stop somewhere for a night, although I don't remember where I stopped. But the second day was also clearly a very long drive, and I did not need a nap that day either.

The lessons continued while I drove. I was taught that every breath can be a temple, as we give thanks for the gift of life, because breathing is a privilege. I was also taught to hold forgiveness in every breath. This came in handy for family gatherings!

Apparently, Buddha was still teaching me to laugh at myself and at life, for he taught me rapidly to repeat the phrase, "Buddha belly, Buddha belly, Buddha belly," which is really hard to do without laughing! It was like a child's game to laugh at something so silly, or maybe you had to be there, and in this level of consciousness where you're actually getting to interact with Buddha himself, to laugh at that. I'm sure that at some levels of ego-consciousness, one would feel that one has to take Buddha seriously, and out of respect, not laugh at all. But that kind of seriousness would only be necessary for someone who has ego. So maybe God can laugh (metaphorically) at God's own Self – I hope so! Or, maybe humor is just something we need to help us let go so we can get to that state beyond it all – Bliss!

The really funny truth is that, although Michele taught me what she tells me now is the Bhastrika pranayama, the way I "learned" it, in my ignorance of all things pranayama back then, was apparently wrong. At least, according to everything I have seen online, and according to the practice of the Bhastrika breath at Power of Breath yoga, which was the same as the practice at a Kundalini yoga class I recently

60

attended, what I ended up doing as a pranayama is not officially taught by anyone that I can find.

I am confident Michele taught it correctly, but I practiced it incorrectly. The most ironic part of it is that, the way I practice this "pranayama" actually helps drive the energy up to my crown chakra, whereas the proper technique of Bhastrika seems to me more generally to energize one's whole self. Or, maybe what I've been doing is just "wrong," and the fact that I hold the intention of energizing the crown chakra creates the effect, since "energy follows intention."[17]

See how useful it can be to laugh at oneself on the spiritual path, and not to take oneself too seriously!

Back to the trip to Texas ... As I drove on this long and challenging trip, I was also taught to have faith and courage, and to persevere. I was taught to serve constantly and lovingly. My consciousness, at this level, became aware of the need for greater compassion, as well as for putting others first constantly.

One of the ways I expressed higher consciousness of putting others first was by frequently walking my sister's dog during this time, as the dog was excluded from some of the family activities. As an empath and an animal healer, I am often unable to tune out the feelings and needs of animals. I had to respond to the dog's needs.

As a family, we had several days together. I had to decide with whom I would share the experience of the "Enlightenment Vision." How do you tell anyone about this without people thinking you are bragging? If they are coming from ego, they may well think so. If they are genuine seekers on the path of Self-Realization, they will respect and honor the experiences of others on the path.

I decided to share it with my young adult son and his fiancée (now his wife). That went easily enough, with neither of them doubting, questioning, or ridiculing. However, it did not seem like the

---

[17] "Energy follows intention." This is a principle known widely in energy healing work, but is more broadly a spiritual truth known through the spiritual science of subtle energy, or life force (prana).

appropriate time to share it with my daughter, although later that summer, the appropriate time did present itself. Nor did I share it with anyone else in my family. In fact, as my parents were declining somewhat mentally, I never did tell them before they died. I have only recently told my niece, and my brother now knows (nearly five years later), but my sister still does not know – at least, I have not discussed it with her.

For the first time I could remember, the family gathering went smoothly in the sense that I did not take anything personally nor did I find it difficult to cope with the family dysfunctions (virtually all families have some level of dysfunction, as I learned in seminary). I believe that non-attachment helped immensely, along with a higher consciousness, complete with a sense of Divine connection.

By the time the family gatherings were at an end, I did not appear to have enough cash to make it all the way home, and apparently I did not have much of the $2,000 left in the bank. My 20-something son actually gave me some cash, which ended up being necessary for paying for gas. I cannot remember if I stayed in a hotel. I do remember resting in a rest area at some point.

As I drove both to and from Texas, I was taught many lessons. What a great way to pass the time while driving 1,300 miles "by yourself," discovering that you are never really and truly "by yourself."

One of the lessons was about the gift of life, expressing more fully why we need to breathe in gratefully the gift of life. The reason that I needed this lesson was that, as a young widow, a single mom, a single woman who desired a partner very much, and a person with chronic pain in my jaw from TMJ[18] and serious knee problems, I had spent about two decades not feeling very fond of "life." I periodically experienced that emotional devastation that includes depression, resentment, anger and self-pity. On one level, I had sometimes felt

---

[18] Temporomandibular joint syndrome, which has much improved through the practice of meditation, energy healing, and attaining more inner peace.

that way; yet on another level, ever since learning to meditate, I had felt glad and joyous and loved meditating and connecting with God.

What I was reminded as I drove was that life is a gift – a good gift. Many years before, when I lived in Nashville, Tennessee, attending Vanderbilt Divinity School, I had a friend who always said, "Life is good." I would object, and say, "Life is not always good, but God is good." He had the wisdom not to argue with me, even though he was "right." I would add that, growing up in Africa, I was well aware that life did not seem "good" for millions of starving people around the world.

From the perspective of the spiritual path of union with God,[19] we constantly receive exactly what we need in life in order to make progress on our spiritual path, or to help someone else make progress on theirs.

Yes, that means that even the "awful," the "horrible," and the "very bad," things that happen to us are just part of what is needed in each moment for our spiritual progress. So we can rejoice – right!? It is not always easy, I *do* know, but yes, we can rejoice.

In every moment, we are receiving the gift of life, just as we need it in order to learn, to let go of ego, or to love and serve God as we help someone else.

If we resent this moment, right now, we are blocking our spiritual progress. If we feel anger, fear, resentment, or even frustration, we are blocking the gift of life, by resisting it in this moment. Each moment that we resist life, whether through resentment or desire, through anger or fear, we block the flow of prana into ourselves as we breathe. When we block the flow of prana, we block the flow of life to ourselves. Mentally blocking the flow of life leads to energetically blocking the flow of life to ourselves, even for our own needs.

---

[19] Or the path of Self-Realization, which is also the path of yoga, for "yoga" means "union" as in "union with God."

Accepting life "as it is" in each moment leads to the continual flow of life force into us, to help us with each and every situation. In order to love life, we have to love each and every moment. Moreover, if we would like to *receive a life we love*, then we need to love life as it is.

So, we can laugh at "me" again that I had to "eat" my own words, and affirm, like my friend in Tennessee, that "Life is good!"

Still driving, another lesson came to me about life. This lesson provided a spiritual understanding of the concept and reality of Life.

Have you ever really wondered what we mean when we say "life"? It's such a nebulous word – a mysterious word, abstract and vague - difficult to pin down to anything concrete and verifiable. There's life in living beings, and then there's this experience we all share called "life." Despite dictionary definitions that use words such as "animate" and "metabolism" and "reproduction," these words seem to *describe* life more than actually *define* the essence of life.

What came to me while driving is that what we refer to casually as "life" is really "Life," with a capital "L." It also came to me that "Life" is actually what Christians tend to call "the Holy Spirit," the third person of the Trinity.

Regardless of our religion or lack thereof, we human beings generally know intuitively that Life is Holy, that Life is sacred.

In actuality, Life is the ever-present Spirit of God acting in the universe to create and to guide life, to empower the created world in general, as well as to empower Divine intentions in particular, in the midst of the chaos we might call reality, or the world.

This led me to reconceive of the Trinity from a more interfaith as well as a gender inclusive spiritual view. First, there is God the Father/Mother, who is beyond the universe, and who is the Source of Life. Life, then, is the vibratory essence of creation.

There is also the Christ, or Buddha, or Consciousness of God, which is the expression, or visible Face, if you will, of the Divine in creation. The concept of Christ, or Divine Consciousness, may be expressed as the visible Face of Grace[20] in action. As I experience the "Christ-Consciousness" within myself (or Buddha-Consciousness, or Enlightened Consciousness, if you prefer), I experience it as a combination of sheer grace and compassion.[21]

This visible Face of God is incarnational - not just spirit, but spirit embodied within people, including, but not limited to Jesus himself. Many holy saints, yogis and yoginis[22], Swamis, and others have attained the same elevated consciousness of both Christ and Buddha. "Christ" is a title, a Greek translation of the Hebrew term "Messiah," which means the "Anointed One," so it originally did not refer only to Jesus. Anointed Ones serve within creation with a visible Face, so that we may see the One (God) who is blessing us.

The third 'person' of the Trinity is the Holy Spirit, or actually, Life. Life is the loving, wise energy (vibratory essence) of the Divine in creation which creates the divinely ordained aspects of our lives. Some people would refer to this as God's Will – Life as Spirit empowers Divine Will to occur as freely as possible.

Within the universe, there exist both freedom and free will. This means that fear-based and hurtful intentions can create painful events which clearly are not God's "will." Hurtful events do happen, and they present themselves in our lives as opportunities for spiritual growth – either for us, or for someone else. But these hurtful events that are created by fear and by a sense of separation from God are not

---

[20] Here, grace means "gift," as in, everything is a gift from God. This kind of gift lovingly accepts, affirms, welcomes and supports us ALL as "children" of the Divine Mother/Father.

[21] I sometimes also express this as Unity Consciousness, just as much as either Christ-Consciousness or Buddha-Consciousness. It also makes sense to express this aspect of God as the Mind of God, or the Consciousness of God as manifested in the universe. For more on this, please refer to the concepts of Sat (Truth), Tat, and Aum, in Hindu thought.

[22] A yogini is a female who seeks union with the Divine through the science of yoga.

directly divinely designed, even though everything is divinely energized.

God's energy is necessary for anything to occur. Without Life energy in the Universe, nothing would exist, and nothing would happen. With God's energy, and the mix of our own fear-based intentions, even negative, hurtful things can happen.

Life acts even in and through those painful events, to bring about divine blessing sooner or later, even if no apparent blessings happen right away. While there is freedom for destructive things to occur, when we trust God, we trust Life. It's always best when we cooperate with Life.

That's not to say that we are to compromise ourselves and cooperate with the world of fear-based, self-serving material motives, but we are to cooperate with the flow of Life, which is loving, wise, and serving others. Life bestows blessings which are meant to be shared.

Paramahansa Yogananda writes in his book, *Autobiography of a Yogi,* about the Trinity, describing God as the "Uncreated" or the "Absolute," who exists beyond this universe, as well as the "Son" or Christ-Consciousness, as the "sole reflection" of the Uncreated, Absolute aspect of God. Also, Paramahansa-ji describes the Holy Spirit as "the only activating force"[23] in the universe.

Yes! The "activating force" in the universe is Life! The Holy Spirit is Life! So, we definitely need to cooperate with Life. This is not the materialistic, hedonistic, self-centered life that we so often find ourselves caught up in. This is Life that directs the flow of divine blessing, and we can choose to be filled with as well as part of that Life.

A beautiful thought that came to me while I was driving was that the unity of the Trinity happens within each one of us when we

---

[23] Paramahansa Yogananda, *Autobiography of a Yogi, (Los Angeles: Self-Realization Fellowship),* copyright 1998, Thirteenth edition, note on p. 169, very much worth reading!

attain Christ-Consciousness or Enlightened Consciousness within. When the consciousness within us attains the level of Christ or Buddhahood, then we are one with our Divine Father/Mother as well as one with the Christ-Consciousness as well as one with the flow of Life (Divine Spirit)!

In that state, our consciousness remains in a state of love, peace, and bliss, and our Lives flow with an ease that comes from embodying sheer grace. That is pure bliss. May we attain this state within ourselves, and among ourselves as well! What a Life that will be to share together – when we are all One with Life!

The next lesson that came to me was the meaning of "blasphemy." This term comes from both Judaism and Christianity – the idea of speaking blasphemy against God. In the current context, what came to me was the idea of "blaspheming the Holy Spirit."

Since the previous intuition was that Life, or the flow of Divine Life in the Universe, is the same as the Spirit of God, then it stands to reason that blasphemy would be doing or saying anything that rejects, denies, takes away from, or puts down Life.

I then remembered that Jesus said the *only unforgivable sin* was blaspheming the Holy Spirit.

Yet, and this is a **super important question**: *How do we understand anything as being "unforgivable" if we believe in grace, non-judgment, unconditional love, and forgiveness?*

Well, I was still driving to Texas (1,300 miles is a long time to drive, giving plenty of time for pranayama-inspired teachings from the Masters), when next, it came to me that when we resist Life, we are actually blaspheming the Holy Spirit, in effect.

In other words, every time we resist Life, whether out of frustration, impatience, resentment, or anger, we are blaspheming Life itself. When we blaspheme Life itself, Life does not yield to our anger or our frustration.

Rather, the negative energy (and negative thoughts that generate that negative energy) block us from receiving the benefits of flowing with Life. *Our negative thoughts are the blasphemy*, and they produce the negative energy, which results in negative, unproductive, unloving, unfruitful results.

In the sense, then, that our resistance to Life creates unfruitful results, we are creating our own lack of forgiveness - the unfruitful results themselves constitute that un-forgiveness.

Life does not yield to negativity.

Life allows negativity, of its own free will, to create unloving results. Just so:

Our negative thoughts are unforgiven in the sense that they create unloving results when we energize them with strong negative emotions.

We, and others, naturally suffer the consequences of those results.

This is, by the way, the essence of karma: reaping what we sow through our thoughts, our intentions, and our energies, as much as through our actions. Resistance to Life through impatience, arrogance, lack of forgiveness, resentment, fear, and anger, all constitute blasphemy.

So, blaspheming the Holy Spirit means resisting what God is doing in the world, and in our lives, even in subtle and often largely unconscious ways. Only when we peacefully go with the flow of Life, rejoicing in all things, are we praising the Holy Spirit at all times.

Please do not misunderstand me as saying that we do not resist injustice or work for change, or accept abuse. As spiritual warriors, we remove ourselves and others from dangerous and abusive situations, we also protect others from injustices, and we work for peaceful changes in our lives and in the world.

And yet, we stand for change and we work for change from a place of inner peace and acceptance, knowing that Life supports those who intend the increase of Love and Justice and Truth in Life. So, as we become part of Life creating more love and life in the world, we continually think, act, and believe in the positive power of Life to create more life and love. As spiritual warriors, we act for change from a place of gratitude for the opportunity to serve Life.

Please understand that there is a difference between Life and Maya. Life is the Divine Spirit which presents us with what we are experiencing. Maya is what we are experiencing. Maya is the illusion we call "reality." Maya has the dual nature of light and dark, good and bad, Presence and Separation, or God and ego. Every part of Maya which we experience as "negative" is temporary.

Life is the Flow of Divine Presence, energizing and empowering all that exists.

Because the negativity of Maya can include poverty, abuse, neglect, injustice, injury, illness, and so on, we who are filled with Light strive to transform these negative aspects of Maya into positive aspects through Divine Presence.

One of the steps in transforming Maya is accepting Life as it presents itself, and being grateful for the opportunity to learn or to serve, to grow, or even to sacrifice ourselves for the greater good.

Acceptance and gratitude are the keys to transforming Maya into a Life worth living. Lack of acceptance along with lack of gratitude blocks the flow of Life in its most positive possibilities. We accept Maya as temporary; we accept, give thanks for, and praise Life as our Teacher.

When we fail to honor Life as our Teacher, we blaspheme the Spirit of God. Anything less than complete and constant praise and gratitude for Life constitutes blasphemy.

When we are called onto the Spiritual Path which leads us to Oneness with God, we are called not only to fall in love with God, but we are also called to fall in love with Life!

Well, this newfound teaching was definitely put to the test right away! I was given what would have otherwise been an unwelcome opportunity to learn this lesson, except, given the lesson, I had to welcome this opportunity to live it.

Driving home from Texas to Michigan, the very end of the trip became a perfect test. There was supposed to have been rain much of the way, but I had kept praying, and the rain had stayed away for most of the trip. (I had had, over the preceding years, multiple answers to prayers for weather, some of which were dramatic). Well, just at the end of the trip, late at night, driving through the Chicago area, it finally began to rain – a real storm.

If you have ever driven along the highways of Chicago, you know how challenging the traffic can be at the best of times, let alone in the rain at night. As I drove into Indiana, the rain got so heavy that I could not even see the lines on the road, which were faint anyway. My windshield wipers were not working well, and my windshield was fogging up. It was dark, as it was about midnight. I could barely see anything other than rain. It was all I could do to keep from driving off the road.

I very clearly had the sense that this was exactly the time to have both faith and courage, and to keep driving. That sense of connection through this new consciousness of a higher Teacher gave me the courage to keep driving, even though it looked and felt impossible to do it safely – and it was late and I felt nearly exhausted.

The message I was given was: "You will have to drive through the storm, but you will make it safely to the other side, and everything will be okay."

I knew that this message was a metaphor for trusting and letting go of fear, even though I was returning home to a possible eviction notice, with no clear idea how to pay my bills or to advance my career. And yet, what I heard to be true was, "Everything will be okay."

And indeed, I made it home safely. And true enough, somehow, everything worked out okay.

I love the Teacher Voice. I love the presence of, or perhaps I need to say, access to this Higher Consciousness. Years later, I came to understand that this access began to occur because of the opening (or energizing) of my crown chakra. What an amazing experience, and how greatly life changed because of it.

Of course, the Raja Yoga meditation and Kriya yoga meditation are designed to open and energize all the chakras, from lower to higher, and the teaching is that, if you practice with faith and devotion, it will happen to you as well. It took me fourteen years of practicing before getting there.

I believe that devotion is the key that unlocks that crown chakra door. Faith helps us rise up from the heart chakra through the throat and Third Eye chakras, but devotion is essential to take us all the way home. Devotion is a way of life, not just a twice-a-day practice.

The energy of devotion is Love.

CHAPTER SEVEN: HEALING WITH THE SEVEN RAYS

The part of the Enlightenment Vision in which I saw light and was told that I had "become one who could channel the Seven Rays for others" still needed some explanation for me to understand the full implications. When I saw the light, my memory is that it was like rainbow flashes of light – like dancing lightning made of prisms of light.

Of course it was a beautiful and moving experience, and yet, I had no idea what it meant to channel the Seven Rays for others, or how to do it. I did sense that it meant there was a purity in me making this possible. (Not that I experience myself as extraordinarily "pure," but I have committed myself to a distinct lack of material desire.)

Since I had learned of the Seven Rays from the Reiki Master who had taught me Reiki levels one and two, I wrote to him by email to ask for information. The man who taught me is John Kroneck, of Spirit of Wellness in Stanton, Michigan.[24] John's initial response was something like "wow!" or "cool!" but he also expressed that the vision deserved time for him to reflect and get back to me with a good answer.

Some time passed before I heard from John again, but it was that summer when I received an email from him with an attachment of a "Chart of the Seven Rays" from the *Law of Life*, Book II. John wrote that the Seven Rays permeate creation, along with two new rays which have been added to bring a higher frequency etheric energy for the spiritual progress of human beings.

Then John expressed trust that I would be able to learn more from the Archangels and Ascended Masters of the Seven Rays. This

---

[24] John Kroneck is the author of the beautifully insightful and informative book, *Reiki Energetics*.

surprised me, but then I realized that, given the vision I had just had, it would make sense that I would be able to connect with the Ascended Masters again, and to learn more from them as well as from the Archangels directly.

So, I began to study the chart, and to pray to the Archangels of the Seven Rays: Michael, Jophiel, Chamuel, Gabriel, Raphael, Uriel, and Zadkiel. I had already been told years before that Archangel Raphael was helping me with the healing work I do. Also, I had been told that Archangel Michael considers me "one of his own," which I later learned meant that he protects me. (Yes, alleluia! What great news is that?!)

What I asked for from the Archangels was guidance to learn how to channel the Seven Rays. Since I had already been asking Archangel Raphael for help with healing, this was not a huge stretch for me, even though I was currently working among Christians who adamantly insisted that one does not pray to angels. Gradually, over time, my prayers to the Archangels have been refined, as I have learned how to pray more and more effectively.

What evolved at that time was a practice of prayer for becoming filled with the Seven Rays, in a specific way physically, devotionally, as well as energetically. For a while, I did the long version of this prayer, although I quickly shortened it to a manageable version for daily morning prayers. And so I began honoring and talking to Archangels on a daily basis – how wonderful is that!?

Since I was not doing very much healing work at the time, the main difference I noticed was that being filled with the Seven Rays brought me such a pure energy of peace and calmness – a higher, lighter vibration.

I also noticed, at times, that animals responded to this beautiful energy in me. While I was accustomed to doing animal healing, and had experienced the healing energy drawing animals to me, I had never before experienced living inside an energy that drew animals toward me during the day. The one possible exception to this was my "coyote story," recounted in my first book, in which a wild coyote trusted me to help remove a plastic jar that it had gotten stuck on its head (one of my favorite stories!).[25]

Well, if I remember correctly, for a few weeks, I managed to pray the whole version of this angelic prayer of the Seven Rays more or less daily, even over a weekend when I spent three days selling fair trade art and jewelry from the Democratic Republic of the Congo at a summer festival in downtown Kalamazoo.[26] The combination of the energy of the Seven Rays and being out at a street festival served to draw a needy pigeon into my life.

It was the second day of the festival, a Saturday, when a pigeon landed on the pavement between the vendors' stalls. Immediately, some children were attracted to it, and out of concern that the children might scare it, I decided to model being nice to the pigeon. A number of people were around, so it was a little crowded, but not too crowded for the pigeon to look for food.

It seemed to be having trouble pecking at food on the ground, so I broke up a cheesy-peanut butter cracker brought by the friend who was helping me, and tossed it near the pigeon. It still had trouble pecking, so I knelt down and crumbled up the crackers right next to the pigeon.

The pigeon pecked a little bit at the crackers, obviously having difficulty seeing or picking up or both – there seemed to be something wrong with one of its eyes. Then, as I was still squatting next to the pigeon, the pigeon fluttered its wings and landed on my head!

Now, I knew from healing with animals that it would just not

---

[25] This is one of my favorite stories, and the lessons that came from it are beautiful as well. The moving story and beautiful lessons can be found as an appendix at the end of *Aging Well ~ Be Your Best Self Forever!*

[26] I had returned to the land of my birth for the first time as an adult in 2005, along with my daughter who was 19 at the time, and after that, she and I began selling fair trade items to benefit the struggling artists of Kinshasa, the DR Congo, as well as literacy programs for women, aiding orphans of HIV, and feeding hungry people in general through both sales and donations.

do for me to freak out, so I remained calm, while several people around me, including the children, immediately freaked out that there was a pigeon on my head. I calmly stood up, and after a few moments, the pigeon slid down onto my left shoulder.

People were taking photos, and strangers would walk up to me and comment that there was a pigeon on my shoulder. I began to have to try to explain why there was a pigeon on my shoulder. I think I said something like, "I do healing with animals, and I think it needs healing," although that was not an easy thing for me to say in this context. One nearby vendor was from West Africa, and he delighted in the pigeon, because he had kept pigeons back home in his country – whether as pets or for food I don't recall.

One male security guard who was walking around the festival stopped and laughed, finding it funny that the pigeon was on my shoulder. We had a fun and friendly conversation.

The pigeon just stayed on my shoulder, even though I was moving about – slowly – even bending over and picking up paintings to show to potential customers. If I tried to turn my head towards the pigeon to look at it, it would peck my cheek, which was painful, so I just gave it its space on my shoulder, and let it be.

At one point, I sat down to rest at the back of the stall, and hoped that the pigeon would fly off my shoulder to either the grass or the tree next to where I sat. It stayed on my shoulder. In fact, it stayed on my shoulder for about two hours.

I knew my daughter and her best friend would be arriving after a while to help with selling the artwork, so I planned to ask my daughter to take the pigeon off my shoulder, because my daughter is naturally gifted with animals. My daughter arrived about two hours after the pigeon got on my shoulder, and it was still there when she called to say she was at the gate.

I had to take wristbands to her and her friend so that they could get in for free to help, so I walked slowly through the festival to the gate, enduring the awkwardness of walking around in public with a wild pigeon on my shoulder. I even saw a state senator whom I knew,

75

a very proper gentleman, to whom I said, "Hello, yes, I know I have a pigeon on my shoulder."

When I arrived at the gate, the woman security guard started yelling at me. "You can't take that bird in there!" *It lives here.* "You can't take that bird in there; there are food vendors in there!" *It's not my bird; it lives here.* "You can't take that bird in there!"

So, I walked out the gate and asked my daughter to get the bird and to place it on a nice little tree nearby. She distracted it with one hand, and gently lifted it with the other, placing it on a low branch where we could all look at each other, and we did. I felt sad leaving the bird, and I missed it that night.

The next day, the friendly male security guard who had enjoyed the fact that the pigeon was on my shoulder came by to tell me that the pigeon had later returned, obviously looking for me, because it kept landing on people's heads and freaking them out. He repeated that the pigeon was looking for me.

I never saw the pigeon again. It blessed me, and I hope and pray that it will always be blessed by the Divine energy of love and light – all seven rays of it!

Despite that experience, I believe it took me awhile to learn how to pray for the Archangels of the Seven Rays to bring through the energy when I do energy healing work, or give people energy healing, whether in person or at a distance. Eventually, though, it became my regular practice to ask for the Seven Rays of healing when doing healing work with people – and sometimes with animals. That definitely seems to have "ramped up" the healing energy coming through me ever since, as well as the benefits people receive, and the intuitions I perceive.

The energy seems purer, lighter, even than the Reiki level two which I had already received, and the Reiki level three which I have since received. To maintain this level, one needs to keep one's own vibration high through eating a vegetarian diet, forgoing alcohol, meditating, praying, and living a life of love, devotion, and compassionate service. At odd times when my vibration has dropped, it has seemed to me to become more difficult to heal at this level, channeling the Seven Rays.

Of course, I am not "doing" the healing; I am just serving as a channel for the healing energy and the intuitive knowing that comes through to help people. God, the Archangels, and the angels of love and light do the healing. Sometimes, people's own guardian angels or Spirit Guides help. Nowadays, I sometimes experience Ascended Masters helping, especially Mother Mary.

The first time that I vividly remember Mother Mary showing up was a couple of years ago, as I was preparing to do an energy healing here in Washington, DC. The woman who was to receive the healing was Spanish-speaking and from South America, so a translator had been arranged, because my Spanish is quite limited. As I was praying to connect with God and the Archangels before the healing, Mother Mary popped into my head. At the time, I thought, "I wonder if the woman is Catholic; since she's from South America that might be expected, and would make sense of why Mother Mary showed up."

When the woman and the translator were in the room, as I was getting to know her and what she needed, I asked the translator to ask if the woman had a faith background from which she draws in her daily life. The translator did so.

The woman apparently responded, "No, I believe in the power of nature."

I thought, well, that's perfect for Reiki energy healing, since the energy is in nature; if she believes in it, great!" Sensing some resistance to religion, I dropped the subject for a moment.

Later, I brought the conversation around to faith again, and mentioned that Mother Mary had appeared to me when I prayed for her before the healing. The translator told her, and the woman replied: "Oh, my mother is Catholic and she prays to Mother Mary for me every day!"

Wow! The woman's mother prays to Mother Mary for her daughter's well-being every day somewhere in South America, and Mother Mary shows up in Washington, DC, to help bring healing to the daughter in answer to the mother's prayers. How wonderful Mother Mary is in this amazing Universe!

Working with the Archangels and Ascended Masters to bring healing to people both in person as well as at a distance constitutes one of the greatest joys of my life. What they accomplish often seems remarkable to me. And the Archangels keep on teaching more about healing, and increasing my intuitive "knowing" to cover more situations and subjects. This has vastly improved both the energy healing and the life coaching work I do. I am truly humbled and extremely grateful.

CHAPTER EIGHT: MY FATHER'S DEATH & THE DESCENT OF CONSCIOUSNESS

After the Enlightenment Vision, I lived, generally, though not every moment, in this elevated state of consciousness for a few months. Then, in late September of 2010, my sister called me to say that our father was dying, and she wanted me to come down to San Antonio to help with our parents. My niece then made arrangements with me, and paid for me to fly down.

I ended up staying in the assisted living home with my parents. This meant that I slept on the love seat, getting up several times at night to help both parents when they went to the bathroom.

There was little opportunity for me to meditate, and I was becoming increasingly exhausted. I did give my father an energy healing, but I could just feel how worn out his body was from working hard and living a life devoted to serving God. I could energetically and intuitively feel that he had earned the phrase, "Well done, good and faithful servant."

Even with all the challenges, my absolutely favorite moments with my parents happened during the middle of the night, when both parents would be awake, and I would crawl into bed between them, and sing hymns and Christmas carols with them, to help them relax and go back to sleep. We did that for at least two nights. The night before he died, my father anticipated and devotedly sang the words of "How Great Thou Art" despite his obvious decline.

When my father died, my sister and niece and I tried to work together to make the funeral arrangements. Of course I had different ideas than they, coming from a more church-oriented background, as church had always been important to my parents as well as to me.

We had a disagreement, an accusation was made, and I burst into tears and came crashing down from that Enlightenment Plateau which I had been enjoying so much for four months. I was just too exhausted, grieving, and lacking the peace of meditation to be able to maintain that higher consciousness at that point. In addition, my "inner wounded child," as we call it in psychotherapy, felt wounded.

Nonetheless, many beautiful spiritual moments occurred throughout this whole time, and I still "heard" the Teacher Voice at times when I needed it most. My favorite occurred when I felt so unknown in my denomination while speaking with my parents' minister, who clearly seemed to be well-known in the denomination.[27] As I listened to her speak, I heard the Higher Ups (the Teacher Voice) say: "Do not be concerned with being accepted on earth, for you have been accepted in heaven." That settled that issue quite well!

We did have a beautiful service for my father, graced by Rev. John Humbert, who was once the General Minister and President of the Christian Church (Disciples of Christ), and who gave part of the eulogy along with me.[28] Two of our parents' dear friends from the Congo came, Georges and Molingo Bokamba, and Georges poured out a libation "to the ancestors," adding that my father was now an ancestor.

That thought really got to me. I was not yet ready to think of my father as an ancestor, but that would be what he wanted – a good memory of him as an ancestor.

Since then, especially through my healing and life coaching work, I have come to a greater understanding of the spirituality of honoring our ancestors, as well as of connecting with them even though they have passed on. Personally, too, however, I have discovered that there are times when one can mystically connect with

---

[27] My parents were missionaries in the Christian Church (Disciples of Christ), and I followed almost in their footsteps by becoming an ordained minister in the Christian Church (Disciples of Christ), known commonly as "Disciples"- always plural to reflect that we do not follow and serve God alone, but rather as a community.

[28] When my father was growing up in Bellefontaine, Ohio, he was active in the youth group of First Christian Church, where John Humbert's father, Rev. Dale Humbert, was the pastor. My father's father had died when he was three, and his mother died during his senior year of high school. Although my dad had already turned 18, the Humbert family took my father in, and claimed him, and therefore us, as family. What grace!

loved ones who have passed on. One can learn from them, and one can even bring healing into relationships with those who have passed on as well.

My father passed away just before his eighty-sixth birthday, on September 21, 2010. After helping with the arrangements, and keeping my mother company for a couple of days, I returned home.

At the end of the summer, my part-time job had ended, and I had applied to substitute teach in the Kalamazoo and Portage public schools. The day after I returned from San Antonio, I started substitute teaching for the first time in my life, without any formal training as a school teacher.

While there is of course a fair degree of excellence in the schools there, I found myself shocked at the condition of schools due to budget cuts, excessively large classroom sizes, and the culture of poverty that pervaded many, but not all, of the classrooms. I witnessed language, behavior, ignorance, and attitudes that were literally shocking to me, as they were completely different than anything I had ever experienced before. The heartache of seeing such cultural deprivation was overwhelming to me.[29]

One exchange student from Europe, observing some of the unacceptable, yet much "milder" misbehavior in a high school class, told me that such behavior would never be tolerated in the schools in Europe (Germany, if I recall correctly), saying that the students would be sent home. I frequently saw far worse behavior, and heard far worse

---

[29] The closest educational comparison I can make from my own recent experience is to schools in East Lansing, Michigan, where my children attended from elementary school through high school, and to the elementary school they attended in an affluent area of Nashville, Tennessee. The contrast is truly significant, largely because of cultural, budget, and economic differences. I felt comfortable as a mom, the times I volunteered in classrooms in both settings.

language.

There are of course, many wonderful students, teachers, and principals in Kalamazoo. I also personally knew the superintendent of schools and knew that he was doing a remarkable job given budget constraints.

My own challenges of arriving early enough to try to understand how to teach the lesson each day, whether for kindergarten or elementary classes, high school classes, middle school subjects, or whatever each day might bring, added immensely to the stress. I generally found myself feeling challenged way beyond my ability to maintain a state of enlightenment.

I do remember a few times when I managed to bring in and through[30] the kind of love needed for these kids, from a healing perspective or higher consciousness level. Other than that, the stress of substitute teaching in the equivalent of an urban school setting primarily exacerbated my struggles with regaining higher consciousness, and instead, ego-consciousness often ruled both my energy and my attitude.

Please understand that I love kids, and that I really enjoy working with children and teenagers in healthy settings, and had often done so in churches. Most of these class settings, though, combined with my being a substitute teacher, were not conducive to frequent positive interactions.[31]

Part of the challenge was that I did not manage to make much time for meditation. Generally, I would receive a 5:30 a.m. phone call

---

[30] This is a phrase which makes sense to people who are accustomed to being vessels of higher energies; I do not know how to explain it to people who have never been aware of Divine Love and Divine energies coming through them for other people, except to say that Divine Love and energy can flow through us for others.

[31] There were some classes and many students with whom I did have positive experiences, of course. The kindergartners at the bilingual school were especially delightful. There were two more affluent schools with new school buildings on the west side of town that were also quite pleasant schools in which to substitute teach.

from the automated substitute placement system, announcing a job availability, and allowing me to accept or reject the job. (I usually accepted.)

Then, in order to manage to get to school on time, after getting ready as quickly as I could, letting the dog out, feeding the cat and dog, and preparing a nutritional smoothie for myself as well as a "sack lunch," I would often only quickly say my prayers and spend perhaps one to five minutes meditating in the morning.

If I were going to an elementary school, I usually had more time, but still, this did not allow the long, forty-five minute or more meditations I needed for reaching higher states of consciousness. Twenty minutes can be good for feeling peaceful and centered, but more than that is generally needed at first to raise our vibration to the crown chakra and above. That lack of meditating makes a huge difference in maintaining higher consciousness.

Clearly, we need to meditate in order to rise above ego-consciousness, and Raja Yoga meditation and Kriya yoga meditation are especially designed to raise our consciousness to higher levels, including Union with God. I fully credit both Raja and Kriya yoga meditation for enabling me to receive the visions as well as the connections with Higher Beings.

Meditating for long periods is essential until we have arrived at the state of *nirbikalpa Samadhi,* which is complete and lasting peace and bliss through union with the Divine. So, at that time, I would do my best to make up for my short morning meditations by meditating longer on weekends.

Since then, I have discovered that, until we have healed our own inner wounded child issues, we cannot remain in an enlightened state all the time. As an intuitive life coach, I am aware that essentially all of us have an inner child that has been wounded to some degree, some more than others. The universe has graciously been working with me diligently for the last two years, to heal the wounds within my own consciousness – on all levels. Healing our inner self is essential for maintaining higher consciousness on an ongoing basis.

I share some of my struggles on the spiritual path in order to show that one does not have to be "special" or to have "special abilities" to learn to work with angels, archangels, and Ascended Masters.

Sharing my own inner weaknesses demonstrates two major points: first, that we must deal with our own baggage rather than hiding it or being in denial about it in order to raise our vibration on the spiritual path to Self-Realization; and second, that God will help us transform and lead us forward on the path if we are willing to be transformed.

One only needs love and devotion to God, a desire to be One with God, a dedication to service, non-attachment to the material world, along with a purity of intention in life. Anyone and everyone is capable of these things; it is simply a matter of awareness, choice, and priorities.

ॐ

CHAPTER NINE: LIFE AS LESSONS IN SELF-REALIZATION

Despite my struggles to maintain higher consciousness during this period of my life, the lessons continued, and the sense of direct connection that I had to the "Higher Ups" often occurred as well. I recognized when the higher consciousness that I experienced as Christ-Consciousness was occurring in me. I also recognized this sense of connection as being direct – more direct to God and to Higher Beings than I had known was possible. That's really the good news I would like to emphasize with you; these connections are possible for all of us.

From the Raja Yoga meditation training, I knew that energizing the Third Eye or Brow chakra would lead to this Enlightened, Buddha-Consciousness or Christ-Consciousness. I also knew that the stage after that was opening the crown chakra and attaining Self-Realization. What I was experiencing was something in-between, or so it seemed, when I was not merely residing back in the old, familiar ego-consciousness.

Nonetheless, I received some amazing intuitions and teachings, which I would like to share, because I believe these lessons illustrate how life can become a series of lessons on Self-Realization. It takes us mere mortals many lifetimes to attain Self-Realization, but once we commit to that path, we are given more intense lessons to help us speed up the process, and our progress.

I recently re-read in *Autobiography of a Yogi* that Paramahansa Yogananda had studied under his guru in a previous lifetime. If he had had a guru in more than one lifetime, no wonder he became Self-Realized! What can become of the rest of us who have not had a guru in a previous life, and who don't have one in this lifetime, at least in person?[32]

I believe this is the primary reason the Ascended Masters would like me to share the message of this book with you: so that, if you have not already, you can learn to connect with Ascended Masters as well, and be guided to Self-Realization from gurus even though they have already ascended. I believe they can guide us to this consciousness from higher up, because I have experienced them helping me get closer and closer. The one aspect of which I can assure you is that it is like rock-climbing up the highest peaks, anything but easy!

I would like to share one of the spiritual teachings that I received during this time. The lesson is called, "Life's Substitute Teacher."

As a substitute teacher, I have been watching the variety of attitudes that kids have toward substitute teachers. Many think they don't have to learn anything "today," because "today we have a substitute teacher." Many don't listen as well as they would listen to their regular teacher. Many resent the sub trying to tell them anything. Moreover, many really resent the sub trying to get them to change their own behavior in order to improve the current situation.

It occurred to me that, if Life is our Teacher, many of us, myself included, sometimes act as if we have a substitute teacher. We whine, and we want to take the day off from learning anything. We want the world out there to change and act differently instead of having to change

---

[32] It is possible to consider Jesus Christ, Buddha, Mother Mary, Lady Kwan Yin, Paramahansa Yogananda and other Ascended Masters as one's guru, even though they exist in an exalted state rather than an earthly state of being. In fact, that is exactly what I am encouraging you to do in this book!

the way we act. We don't pay attention to the lessons we could be learning, because we just want to have fun and goof-off with our friends. Or, we resent the substitute life teacher getting in our face and expecting us to learn something, when clearly we think we don't have to. We ignore the fact that our future spiritual path might need us to learn something today.

Oh, yes, hard as it is to admit, as I've watched the various dysfunctional, rude, and hurtful reactions I've received from dozens, if not hundreds of children and teenagers, I have been made aware that I, too, sometimes react to life as if it is a substitute teacher.

Life is our teacher every day. Technically, there are no days off on the spiritual path. Maybe that's why Jesus gave warnings about our souls needing to be ready and needing to watch, and so on. There's a spiritual life lesson around every corner, if only we are willing to receive it.

Each of us needs to ask ourselves questions like: "Am I willing to learn something new today?" "Am I willing to change my behavior instead of simply wanting the world around me to change?" "What am I responsible for today?" "How can I show my respect and appreciation for life today?" "How can I be part of creating a greater good, instead of just living for myself today?"

When we live life with an open and willing attitude, accepting each situation we face with peace, we can learn all that we are meant to learn on our spiritual paths.

There is no substitute teacher in life. The teacher is Life. Life is our Teacher. We simply need to give it our thanks. Life is teaching you - and me - are we grateful?

ॐ

The Rainbow Warrior

Another lesson I learned while substitute teaching was the lesson of being a Rainbow Warrior, which is based on the concept of the Seven Rays of Creation, and the seven Archangels of the Seven Rays, and the virtues that each ray represents. Here then, from my blog at the time, is the lesson of "The Rainbow Warrior."

I was asked to share a lesson about being a Rainbow Warrior. The sign of a rainbow is, as you know, a sign of hope. That hope is also designated by the proverbial "pot of gold at the end of the rainbow." What the pot of gold symbolizes, in spiritual terms, is the ultimate blessing of Divine Will occurring in a person's life.

A Rainbow Warrior protects people's "pots of gold." In other words, a Rainbow Warrior helps people protect their God-given dreams and visions in order to make them come true.

How does a Rainbow Warrior do this? Well, first, we need to understand that the rainbow symbolizes the light of the Seven Rays of Creation, those angelic rays of energy that emanate from God into the universe.

* ❖ *Blue symbolizes Divine Will;*
* ❖ *Yellow symbolizes Divine Wisdom and Divine Power;*
* ❖ *Pink (not a 'normal' rainbow color - I know) symbolizes Divine Love;*
* ❖ *White (again, not a 'normal' rainbow color) symbolizes Hope and Purity;*
* ❖ *Green symbolizes Truth, Science (or True Knowing), and Divine Healing;*
* ❖ *Yellow/Gold represents devotion to the Divine and ministering to others;*

❖ *Purple represents Freedom and Ordered Service.*

A Rainbow Warrior allows all of these Divine light energies to enlighten them; that is, to shine within them to transform them into something greater than themselves. Next, a Rainbow Warrior allows the Rainbow energies to shine through them to transfix the reality of others into something greater, holier, and more purified.

For example, a Rainbow Warrior protects the pot of gold by aligning herself or himself with Divine Will. Aligning ourselves with the Will of God on a daily basis is the only way to accomplish God's ultimate goals and our God-given dreams and visions for our lives. Also, a Rainbow Warrior protects pots of gold by remaining in a consciousness of unconditional love. This requires letting go of both judgments and assumptions.

In fact, unconditional Love calls Rainbow Warriors to understand that Divine Love defines success as: "Everyone gets to become the person they were created to be." Since that is love's definition of success, then one major way in which we can bless others is to help them become the person they are meant to be. As Rainbow Warriors, let us ask ourselves: "Is there something I can do today to help someone else become the person they are meant to become?"

Ultimately, a Rainbow Warrior begins to find herself or himself transformed by the energies of these virtues and higher intentions, such that we find the Divine Light more fully realized inside us. We discover our God-Self, or "Who God Is" inside ourselves.

It could be said that all of us are trekking along through life like Dorothy and her companions - the Lion, the Tin Man, and the Scarecrow, in "The Wizard of Oz" movie. In the early stages of our spiritual paths, we are all, in essence, traveling through the Land of Oz seeking the god we hope to find outside of ourselves who will bestow gifts we think we lack inside ourselves. Just like Dorothy, the Tin Man, the Lion, and the Scarecrow, our spiritual journeys lead us to discover that we already have a heart and brains and courage, along with other God-given gifts.

We become Rainbow Warriors when we begin to find that God is within us, and the answers are ALL within us. We have no need to travel to find answers, for the Ray of True Knowing is within us. We may travel in life in order to learn, and traveling to learn may open a portal to wisdom and knowledge for us, but the doorway of our mind must be open as well. Indeed, travel becomes unnecessary when we discover that the real portal to Truth is through our own higher consciousness, in fact, through our crown chakras.

Learning to access that higher consciousness through our chakra system, especially through the brow chakra and the crown chakra, is a central aspect of becoming a Rainbow Warrior.

Rainbow Warriors are we, or at least what we will be one day. First, we need to learn to work with the Rainbow energies, or angelic energies, so that we can find the Wisdom we need within ourselves. Raja Yoga Meditation leads us to this well of inner wisdom. This inner wisdom will lead us to those pots of gold, spiritually speaking – those dreams and visions, and a solid sense of Divine Will for our lives, as well as for the lives of others.

Of course, the ultimate pot of gold is union with the Divine Life, the Divine Mind, the Divine Light. May you become your own Rainbow Warrior, ever protecting and pursuing the pot of gold at the end of your rainbow!

"Falling in Love with God."

Have you ever fallen in love with God? In secular cultures, that idea sounds quite strange, the first time we hear it. I once heard that one of the early leaders in my denomination equated salvation with falling in love with God. That idea probably would not have made sense to me until the last year or so, which is when I first remember hearing that idea. (Sometimes, I think we can 'hear' an idea without really hearing it, because we simply are not ready to understand it.)

What does it mean to fall in love with God? Well, for many of us, the word 'God' might get in the way when we begin to consider what falling in love with the divine might mean. There can be too many negative associations with the idea of God, such as an angry God who judges us and who sees us as falling short of God's plan a lot of the time. Or a very masculine, domineering sort of God might lurk in our minds; one who constantly tells us what to do and then reprimands us when we don't do it. Or a God who is never there for us when we need God to help us.

Perhaps you do not have any such negative ideas of God, either consciously or hidden away in your subconscious mind. Either way, let's try substituting the word 'love' for God, and see what happens. The question then becomes: have you ever fallen in love with Love? Divine Love is an amazing and wonderful thing.

Divine Love loves us unconditionally, yet loves us enough to ask us to allow Love to transform us into Love's own image. Love loves us gently, yet with considerable discipline and determination. When we allow Love to fill our hearts and minds and lives; when we begin to see Love all around us; when we see Love in others; then we begin to realize that we actually do love Love.

91

When Love becomes everything to us, in each moment of life, then we realize that we have indeed fallen in love with Love.

Strange sounding, perhaps, but this is truly possible. This falling in love with Love which is "Who God Is" enables us to receive all the love we need for ourselves, and more than enough to share with others. Each day becomes a journey of finding and sharing Love and celebrating it all along the way.

Wouldn't every day become a miracle, if only we would find, share, and celebrate Love all day long? May it be so!

"Forms and Patterns."

As I was walking through the woods with my dog one morning, I felt as though both Eckhart Tolle's writing and Buddha himself were walking with me. In A New Earth, Tolle writes about how what we gain our sense of identity by identifying with forms, but that our true identity is not these forms.[33]

In other words, we really aren't the identity we think we are, because we just base that identity on forms or roles that are temporary in life, but which are not who we really are. All those forms and roles are based on thoughts, and thoughts come from our ego self. Who we

---

[33] For more exposition on this subject, please see: Tolle, Eckhart, *A New Earth: Awakening to Your Soul's Purpose*, (New York: Plume), 2006, p. 56 and the whole book, really! Tolle employs the term "Presence," but I first read this term as a teenager in a little booklet called "The Practice of the Presence of God," by a medieval monk named Brother Lawrence. Versions of this writing appear to be widely available on the internet.

are is an intangible oneness with Presence, the Great I Am of God.[34]

When we identify with these temporary forms, we are tempted to think of ourselves as either better or worse than other people. But none of us is better or worse than anyone else. We all are made of ego and Presence. We just exist in this world as expressions of Divine Presence in and through different forms.

As I was walking through the woods, it dawned on me that many forms combine together inside me to make patterns, and I can simply be grateful for the patterns. For instance, the gift of having lived in different countries while I was growing up created some amazing, diverse patterns in me. I'm so grateful for those patterns, but I also acknowledge that those patterns came from outside of me, came together inside of me, but are not "me." That's when I felt Buddha's presence affirming that this is the path of 'no-self.'

I've never before actually felt capable of accomplishing the degree of 'no-self' called for in Buddhism, but this idea of forms merging into patterns inside us which can be appreciated but not seen as being the same as our 'selves,' makes sense to me. The patterns don't form a 'self,' they are just patterns. By letting the patterns be patterns rather than seeing them as being ourselves, we can not only be grateful for them, but we can also decide more lovingly when to use them, and when to let go of them. This feels incredibly freeing.

And somewhere, Buddha is laughing!

---

[34] These teachings are essentially universal on the mystical path; Paramahansa Yogananda writes similarly about our true identity in God. In addition to his autobiography, I recommend: *Where There Is Light*, (Los Angeles: Self-Realization Fellowship), 2000.

"Temples Everywhere!"

I believe it was on a Self-Realization Fellowship calendar that I read a quote of Paramahansa Yogananda saying that flowers are temples to the Divine Spirit. Perhaps that is why flowers look and often smell so beautiful!

Also, The New Testament tells us that our bodies are temples of the Holy Spirit.[35] Indeed, it is the Divine within us that is our true identity.

Recently, I encountered this idea of temples in two devotional readings on the same day. First, in The Coming of the Cosmic Christ, Matthew Fox wrote about including our bodies, and highlighting them in worship services as a way of connecting our bodies with the cosmic Christ.[36]

Raja Yoga and Kriya Yoga Meditation do this naturally, in the sense that we change the energy of our bodies, and through the chakra system, become a temple of Divine Presence.

In Autobiography of a Yogi, I also re-read the section on J.C. Bose, the famous Indian scientist and inventor whom Paramahansa Yogananda met while he was a youth. Yogananda recounts Bose's speech on the occasion of opening his scientific laboratory, in which Bose announces that the research center was also a temple.[37]

---

[35] 1 Corinthians 3:16, and 6:19.

[36] Fox, Matthew, *The Coming of the Cosmic Christ*, (New York: HarperCollins), 2008. This book was one of two books I was reading when I had my "enlightenment vision," and was extremely helpful and influential at that time and place on "my" path.

[37] Yogananda, Paramahansa, *Autobiography*, p. 79.

*Wow! What would happen in Western culture if we began to
see everything, including scientific laboratories, as temples to the Divine
Creator of us all? What kind of consciousness would we be experiencing
if we began to see everything and everyone as a temple of the Divine?*

*In some cultures road-side shrines are more common than in the
United States. I remember seeing one such shrine on a little Greek
island with very few tourists when we traveled there when I was 17.
Also, the village in which my parents lived in equatorial Africa when I
was born had a shrine just outside the village. Theoretically then, it is
possible for humans to be able, both individually and corporately, to see
everywhere as a potential shrine to Divine Spirit. After all, Divine
Spirit is everywhere. What if everything and everywhere became a
temple in our thinking?*

*Standing in front of the refrigerator would become a
temple. (That could be a hard one for many of us – we're not worshiping
the food!) Our cars would become a temple, and driving would become
an act of worship (no more calling out other drivers, then!). Sitting at
the computer would be choosing to log onto a temple site
(metaphorically), and every internet exchange would express our
gratitude and faith and goodwill and service to the Divine.*

*I realize that at this point, some readers may begin to think of
me as hopelessly idealistic. I grant you that from the perspective of the
material world, it is so. However, when one resides within a
consciousness that is a temple of Divine Spirit, this view of reality
becomes only natural.*

*Indeed, what if every breath became a shrine? I truly believe
that every breath is meant to be an act of worship. Yogic practices have
included breath-work for thousands of years, because every breath we
breathe draws in the life energy of God.*

95

As these intuitive insights came to me, my higher guides were repeatedly telling me to do "pranayamas." Pranayama means "conscious breathing." As we breathe, we can be aware of breathing in Divine Energy — the very Spirit of God — and we can give God our thanks and praise.

In Hebrew, the word 'Ruach' means both 'breath' of God and 'spirit' of God. So, let us breathe, and in doing so, allow God's very Essence to enter us. If we worship God and breathe in God's Presence with every breath, then even we can become true temples of Divine Presence. May it be so!

CHAPTER TEN: LESSONS IN HIGHER CONSCIOUSNESS

My whole life, my mother taught me what she perceived as the true and pure aspects of the teachings and example of Jesus Christ. She embodied many of them herself, especially service, empowering those who are in need, unconditional love, and forgiveness. Both of my parents really modeled these things in ways or to a degree that I have only rarely seen in others. So, in essence, I was raised with aspects of Christ-Consciousness, or higher levels of Divine Consciousness.

Clearly, I still had (and have!) a lot to learn, as God and the Ascended Masters are still teaching me. I am so grateful for these lessons. Here follow some of these early lessons, which generally came to me intuitively, although at the time, reading spiritual books and listening to sermons often prompted further expounding of lessons on the part of the Higher Ups. At some point, we arrive at just knowing – the crown chakra opening seems to lead to this state of knowing beyond ordinary knowing or believing, as though we are already One with Divine Consciousness.

Here then, are more "lessons."

Healing Journey – Homeward Bound

Our lives are a journey from God, back to God, with God and within God all in one. Our ultimate healing is our reunion with God; some might call that our awakening. For some people, the fullness of that awakening does not come until another lifetime; indeed, other people believe that the fullness of that reunion awaits them 'in heaven.'

I attended a funeral today, a home-going celebration for a ninety-year-old African American woman who was hailed as a true servant of

97

God. The pastor's eulogy included some wonderful thoughts, within one phrase that caught my attention: honoring that she is now "at home with God."

I found myself thinking, but what if we feel at home with God right here and right now?

Ultimately, we are most at home when we experience ourselves as being within the Divine Presence. (Our egos may prefer to be away from God, but our souls selves are at home in God.) I believe that our egos are the only things that separate us from God, because that is what our egos believe: that we are separate from God, but this is just an illusion – part of Maya. Or, as the Bible states: "nothing can separate us from the love of God."[38]

In fact, the Bible even refers to "God, in whom we live and move and have our being."[39] This is a very feminine image of God, for the only time we live and move and have our being inside someone else is when we are in the womb! So, Shakti, the Divine Mother, holds us within her womb all the time – we just need to wake up enough to realize that this is in truth where we are!

We can experience Divine Presence in the here-and-now. We are healed by letting go of everything else, and choosing to be One with Divine Presence. In other words, when we choose to allow our Higher Selves, the Buddha, or the Christ presence to reign within us rather than our egos, then we truly experience the Oneness that comes from having the peaceful presence of Divine Spirit, or the "peace of Christ" within (or the peace of Enlightenment).

---

[38] My paraphrase of Romans 8:38-39.

[39] Acts 17:28

Our egos constantly ride a roller-coaster of emotion – up and down with the tides of change in our lives. Instead of experiencing all that turmoil, we can choose to allow the light of Buddha-Consciousness or Christ-Consciousness to energize us to rise above the emotional upheavals – good or bad, and simply choose to be at peace.

Let us be at peace within, and then we will be able to be at peace with one another. We seek the healing presence of divine love within us not just for ourselves, but also for one another. Letting go of our egos is the healing we need, for only by letting go of that which separates us from Divine Love will we be able to experience the healing presence of that unconditional love for ourselves. Only when we allow unconditional love to heal us, will we be able to allow it to heal others through us as well.

When we stop allowing our egos to separate us from the love of God, then we realize that we have attained a sense of being at home on our journey. Love is our home. Love is an energy which is manifested through acts of kindness, words of respect, service to others, courage and other positive intentions and expressions, and so on. Each moment that we choose to let go of ego and to live in the Presence of Divine Love for this moment, we find ourselves at home. This is the healing journey: learning to let go of ego and live in the Divine Love of this moment and every moment. When we live in Love, we are home.

By living in Love, we can be at home and be on the journey at the same time. Living in Love, we can choose to share that love with others. When we live to share that unconditional Love, the journey will be not only healing, but beautiful as well! May Love heal us, may Love bless us, and may Love bring us home!

ॐ

99

Attunement to Holy, Loving Wisdom

Sometimes we confuse the ego-state of making good and reasonable choices with the wisdom of the soul. There is a level of wisdom which the ego can attain, from a purely rational sense.

However, the wisdom of which we speak may have no rational reference point, because it is guided by attunement, and makes choices in faith, even without being able to 'see' the probable outcomes nor the parameters which affect those choices. Living in tune with this holy, loving wisdom becomes a way of life, not just a series of choices.

This level of wisdom reflects a state of consciousness which cannot be attained purely through the rational mind. Attunement is when the heart, the mind, and the gut align with a sense of Love and Truth, free of fear.

Attunement begins with the intention of knowing and living in alignment with Divine Will, or sacred intentionality. This kind of attunement occurs generally when we attain very pure intentions of giving, serving, and loving, all without conditions or expectations of return on our giving, or serving, or loving. This level of living feels incredibly freeing! And blissful!

When we are attuned, the wisdom of the soul brings a constant flow of the energy of peace, and life begins effusively to effect a certain harmony, despite the appearance of challenges as before.

Christ-consciousness and Buddha-Consciousness are names for this constant state of attunement to holy, loving wisdom. May you be blessed with attunement to the Divine Will and the Presence of Divine

Light and Love within you - for a moment, and for a lifetime!

ॐ

Know Thyself

Do you know who you truly are? At first blush, our egos eagerly want to answer, "Of course I do!" But I hear God asking us, "Do you know the truth of who you are?" This divinely-ordained question is much like the ancient Greek oracle's advice: "Know thyself."

If we are to know our Oneness with the Divine, we also need to know ourselves — fully, truthfully, without blinders on, free of shame and blame, with compassionate understanding, forgiveness and grace. Being One with God means healing all that is wounded — that is, healing "all that is not Love" within ourselves.

Knowing the truth of who we are means knowing our full intentions toward everything and everyone. This kind of knowing requires what twelve step programs call a "fearless moral inventory." Our subconscious minds have motives and intentions of which we are often unaware. It takes prayer, feedback from others, and a deeply held commitment to seek out the truth of who we are in order to find all those buried or half-buried unkind thoughts that lurk around in our heads.

It also requires stillness, and adequate time to prepare ourselves to accept the truth of what we find within. We may have deep longings that feel thwarted, and so we may have hidden resentments about what we have not yet done in life. We may have unconscious blame for others because of our thwarted dreams or longings.

101

We may have unconscious fears that we hide from everyone else, and most of the time from ourselves. If we have any anxiety at all, any worries at all, then we have some hidden fears lurking around in our subconscious minds. If we ever, and I mean ever feel nervous, then we have unconscious fears.

Our egos don't want us to know or deal with the truth of our fears, blame, resentments, and hurtful intentions. Our egos want us to think that we will actually protect ourselves by worrying, by blaming someone else, by wishing someone else will fail where we will succeed, or what-have-you.

In order to know ourselves fully and truthfully, we do need to become aware of what our egos have buried in the backyard of our subconscious mind. To accomplish this kind of inner knowing, please note that we will be most effective in the following ways:

❖ *Uncovering our fears will only happen if we devote ourselves to Love (God).*

❖ *Uncovering our blame for others will only happen if we devote ourselves to accepting personal responsibility.*

❖ *Uncovering our resentments will only happen if we dedicate ourselves to being at peace with Life, with ourselves, with others, and with God.*

❖ *Uncovering our hurtful intentions will only occur if we devote ourselves entirely to holding only intentions of love and service.*

As I write this, I hear the intuitive message, "Intention is everything." Those who are "pure in heart" before God are pure in their intentions; they embody the sacred heart of God within themselves.

102

Shakespeare wisely wrote: "To thine own self be true, and it must follow as the night the day, thou can'st not then be false to any man."

If we know the truth, the full truth of who we are, then we will learn to be true to ourselves. Once we learn to be true to ourselves, we will be true to God and everyone else. As Jesus said, "Those who worship God must worship in spirit and in truth." Here, 'in spirit' may be understood as including, but not limited to, those ephemeral aspects of being such as intentions, dreams, desires, and so on.

If we would like to purify our intentions to be able to let go of ego-based, mostly hurtful motivations, and choose to live only by pure intentions of love and light, then we would do well to pray and ask for help. God is only too willing to reveal the truth of ourselves to us. That is the masculine side of God; the truth revealed, not for punishment, but so that we will judge ourselves, and realize our own worthiness or unworthiness. Only we can really change our intentions and worth before God.

At first, we do need to ask for grace to receive forgiveness for and cleansing from those hurtful intentions which we have held somewhere inside ourselves. That's part of worshiping God in spirit and in truth - acknowledging that God alone can forgive and cleanse. We make the choice to change our intentions, but then God helps us do so. Otherwise, we would get stuck in our karma for a long time.

That's also where Christ and other Enlightened Masters come in: they can forgive our karma. When we reach this state of Oneness with God ourselves, we know we are one with Divine forgiveness within ourselves, and so we are able to release karma along with being one with the loving energy and intention of forgiveness.

Forgiveness frees us to move forward on our spiritual journeys.

103

As we move forward, we begin to see Divine Love and grace and forgiveness everywhere, because we have increasingly cultivated the Presence of Unconditional Love and grace within ourselves. The more we empty ourselves in order to be filled with the Presence of God, the more we see God in ourselves, in everyone, and everywhere.

I remembered the words of Jesus: "Blessed are the pure in heart, for they will see God."[40] I began to laugh in sheer bliss! Once we purify ourselves of all the intentions that are not of love, and once we heal all the wounded parts of ourselves, we see and experience God more easily within ourselves, in others, and everywhere — indeed, the pure in heart see God!

Do you know the truth of who you are? When we know the truth of who we are, no one else can ever take that away from us, even though they might never (in this lifetime) see the truth of who we are.

When we become aware that someone is not seeing us for who we are, then we know that they are seeing us through the eyes of their ego. We need to pray for them, and be patient with them. And we simply need to be ourselves for them, even if they don't understand who we are or what we're doing. As long as our intentions serve the highest good, all will be well.

May all be well with you - the real, true You!

---

[40] Matthew 5:8. For virtually all Biblical references in this book, I depend upon the New Revised Standard Version of the Bible, out of gratitude for its use of gender inclusive language for human beings. My personal copy is *The Green Bible*, (San Francisco: HarperOne), 2008. www.greenletterbible.com

Off-Track from the #1 Priority of Life

I trust the wisdom that comes to me, even though I sometimes feel confused by the unknowns that don't yet make sense to me. Rarely content to leave things at the point of thinking, "It's just a mystery and it always will be until we die," I tend to ask God questions, relentlessly, perhaps.

And so, since I ask questions with faith that I will receive answers, I often actually get answers. Sometimes it is difficult discerning wise intuitions from random thoughts that seem to pop into my head. For the most part, though, ever since the vision, I had felt really connected to God, and was receiving wise teachings quite regularly, throughout the day each day. Again, I believe this was a result of Raja and Kriya yoga meditation leading to the opening of my Third Eye and crown chakra.

But then the wise teachings seemed to stop. Worse yet, when I awoke one Saturday morning, and said my post-enlightenment, first-thing in the morning prayers, something did not feel right. Worst of all, when I went to the farmer's market later that morning, I found myself saying something to someone from sheer ego.

*Ouch! That hurt! I guess there's some comfort to be found in realizing that I had come so far in 'practicing the Presence' or 'being the Presence,' as Eckhart Tolle would say,[41] or 'being **in** the Presence' as it felt to me. Mostly, however, I felt horrible, as though my best friend were gone and I had no idea how to get back together with him or her*

---

[41] Tolle, *A New Earth*, a book which I highly recommend reading as part of the path of Self-Realization.

again.

The voice of the Teacher, the wise One who had been teaching me about what to do with pranayamas and so forth, was silent.

I would have felt abandoned except I knew that this horrible sense of separation meant that I had done something wrong. I just had no idea how I had gotten so far off-track. And this happened to be a day when I had the opportunity to preach — just "filling the pulpit" for a Sunday.

What's really awful is when you have to preach and you're not feeling centered. At least to me, I only really enjoy preaching when I find myself "in the flow" of Divine Spirit, led by and filled with and speaking on behalf of the Holy Spirit within me. As I preached this morning, it wasn't that bad, but while I had already prayed to be filled with divine spirit, I forgot to ask for the Holy Spirit in my prayer before the sermon. When have I ever forgotten to ask for the Holy Spirit?!

Actually, the sermon went well enough, and I appreciated the people of the congregation, and generally, a pleasant time was had by all.

Later that afternoon, after doing some pranayamas, but still needing a nap because I had stayed up late working on the children's moment, I started to clean house before the spiritual book study group.

That was when it came to me why I had gotten thrown off-track, as it were. I was told that I had chosen to do pranayamas with the intention of healing the scleritis in my eye, and that this goal had become the number one priority in my life.

In other words, God had no longer become the number one priority. So the sense of onenesss and the Teacher's intuitions had left me, because my priorities were self-serving. Worse yet, my focus had been on the idea that if my eye were healed by the pranayamas, then my

"Aging Well" book could become really popular if I added that into it.

Oh, for pure, God-centered, and God-given intentions! It had come to me that the reason Lady Kwan Yin had marked my head with a red oval was in part to signify the purity of my intentions.

And now I had blown it - the purity of intentions was gone! Ouch!

Well, I thank God that when the Teacher Voice returned, and showed me the error of my intentions, the Teacher voice stayed with me, continuing to instruct me. I was taught that Self-Realization can only be attained through a pure motivation, and that motivation is to be one with love, not in a selfish way, but as an act of service and selflessness.

One cannot misuse the purity of prana and become Self-Realized. Prana is part of what Christians mean by the name the Holy Spirit, and as such, one cannot blaspheme it or one suffers the consequences. In my case, that meant separation from the Divine Self.

Thank God for forgiveness and grace and the opportunity to start over again. When we get off-track, we just need to ask for forgiveness, and then push the re-set button and try again.

The good news, though, is that seeking to be one with Love is a joyful and rewarding experience, because, although one cannot seek it for one's own ends, becoming one with Love does bring more love and healing for oneself. It's automatic.

So, here's to Love: may you find the purity of intentions that lead you to being one with Love in your life, and we will all be united in that Love someday. May Love bless you!

ॐ

Christianity and Self- Realization, Part I

That same night after I was shown the necessity of pure intentions of seeking Unity with God, our spiritual book discussion group raised the question: "Is it possible, through Christianity, to attain Self-Realization?" Two of us gave answers affirming that it is possible to go far on the spiritual path, but that, as long as Christianity is understood as salvation through Jesus as the Christ, external to oneself, rather than through Christ within oneself, one remains unable to take that final step.

This morning, the Teacher started to teach me again. My eye was red again. So, I was shown in no uncertain terms that I need to choose God alone, rather than focusing on the benefits of growing closer to God. I expressed my longing for oneness with the Divine, and gave my whole self, my life, my being, my body, my mind, my soul, to God.

A little while later, after showering, God/the Teacher asked me: "What is the purpose of your life?" I immediately answered: "To love and serve you." There was a spiritual silence in my head, giving me time to realize the unspoken question, "What happened to becoming united with the Divine?"

I realized I had a dilemma, or so I perceived. Which was the purpose of my life, I wondered, to become one with God, or to love and serve God? I guess I had to ask the question in order to receive the answer: "Won't you be able to love and serve me better if you are one with me?"[42]

The answer to that question seems to be an obvious "Yes!" So, the goal of my life is to become one with God that I may better love and serve God.

In Christianity, one holds the goal of serving and loving and glorifying God. Christianity also speaks of accepting Jesus into one's heart, or accepting Jesus Christ as one's Savior, which seems to be in the place of becoming one with God.

What if, all these years, we have misunderstood the intention of "accepting Christ" as one's Savior? What if the intention, instead, was to hear him teaching us to become one with God, even as he was one with God (and still is, of course!)? When Jesus said "I and the father are one, no one comes to the father but by me," he meant that we all need to attain Christ-Consciousness within in order to become one with God just as Jesus became one with God through attaining this higher "Christ" Consciousness.

After all, Christ is not Jesus' last name; Christ is his title. Jesus does not have to be the only one with the title of Christ. And yet Christian tradition has made him so in the minds of millions. That does not mean that we have to continue the tradition.

A Self-Realization perspective on the gospel of Jesus Christ would suggest that we can all indeed attain union with God. A Self-Realization perspective would also suggest that the Biblical teaching,

---

[42] The Teacher Voice, the Ascended Masters when they work with me individually, and the "Higher Ups" in general (when I cannot identify any specific one, that is how I usually refer to them) often teach me through the use of questions. How else can we master ourselves, unless we are able to answer the most important and challenging questions of life? If they gave us the answers, we would just be parrots, or good students, but not necessarily masters. Masters find the answers within.

*"Unless you turn and repent, you will not enter the kingdom of God,"
means that we have to let go of our ego selves in order to become one with
God. "I am the way, the truth and the life," refers to the Great I AM,
or the Divine Presence which is within us all. Jesus was calling us to
find the Great I Am within ourselves, and yet we misunderstood and
followed him instead! Perhaps we followed him because it's easier and
feels safer to be a follower than to do the spiritual work ourselves, or
perhaps because we were not yet ready to understand.*

*As I was getting dressed that morning, all the while in
conversation with God, I decided to wear my huge silver "clergy" cross
on a necklace. The Teacher said to me: "the cross is the way of no-
self." I like that interpretation, but I wondered, "So what happened
to forgiveness?" (As in, the teaching that Jesus died on the cross so that
we might be forgiven of our sins.)*

*The answer that came to me was: "Whenever you let go of your
lower priorities and choose oneness with God, there is a karmic blessing
which includes forgiveness."*

*The way of no-self is now what the cross means to me. And
when we choose no-self and oneness with God, we automatically choose
love and forgiveness for ourselves and others. That IS the way of Christ.*

Christianity and Self-Realization, Part II

*It has become clear to me that there are three basic, big steps on
the path to Self-Realization. The first is enlightenment, which is a way
of seeing. The second is attaining one level of Christ-Consciousness,
which is a way of knowing, followed by living out that "knowing" of*

Christ-Consciousness. The third is attaining Self-Realization, which is a way of being. Our activity, or our doing, which includes, of course, our speaking, arises out of our seeing, knowing, and being.

In other words, at whatever level we find ourselves, we either see and know and do out of ego and ego-based perceptions and motivations, or we see and know and do out of enlightened perception, or out of unconditionally loving omniscience.

When we are in ego, a person may speak or act in a certain way, and we will perceive it as coming from ego, because that is where we are. However, the person might have been acting or speaking out of a purity of their souls, with pure motives, and holy intentions. It is just that other people cannot see the pure intentions if we ourselves fail to hold such pure intentions as well.

Sometimes, a person's actions are so astoundingly loving and self-giving, that we can see the purity of them even though we ourselves may be steeped in ego. That is why the world needs people who give themselves bravely to save someone else's life, and those who donate unbelievably generously to those in need at great sacrifice to themselves, as well as those who are Christ-like by being humble servants.

It is only when actions are so Christ-like that they cannot be missed that the actions break through our usual perceptions from the eyes of our egos. Otherwise, we tend to interpret everything as being ego-based, even when it is not.

Various religions have different ways to help us raise our vibrations, and our consciousness. Most religions include religious rites of worship and prayer.

Christianity in its more charismatic expressions includes inviting the Holy Spirit into one's self in order to be "Spirit-filled." This is a partial act of enlightenment. When done with the

111

understanding that Christ is separate from ourselves, it yields only a partial enlightenment, with perhaps the receiving of spiritual gifts and abilities. Without getting rid of ego, though, this Holy Spirit level of enlightenment is not full enlightenment, because the ego remains and partially blocks the higher levels of spiritual vibration.

Christianity does invite one to let go of ego, and to have purer motivations, to be humble and so on. This process is called sanctification and helps one attain many degrees of Christ-Consciousness. For example, Christians who hold the ideal of self-less, humble service exhibit one of the karmic attributes of Christ-Consciousness. Christians who hold to the ideal of generosity and personal poverty embody another aspect of Christ-Consciousness.

However, all of this stops short of the Hindu concept of Self-Realization unless, perhaps, one is a nun or monk in a convent or monastery, and one has such visions that one is led not only to enlightenment, but also to attaining Christ-Consciousness and Self-Realization. I believe that Christian saints such as Teresa of Avila, Julian of Norwich, and Hildegaard of Bingen quite possibly achieved Christ-Consciousness and Self-Realization — Meister Eckhart clearly did so.

I keep referring to degrees of Christ-Consciousness. This morning, the Teacher made it clear to me that, because of God's universal law of free will, God cannot just give one Christ-Consciousness or make one automatically Self-Realized.

In order to attain a fullness of Buddha-Consciousness or Christ-Consciousness within, one has to purify one's motives and intentions. This is where I went astray with my desire for physical healing. Christ-Consciousness also includes humility, generosity, *poverty,[43] and loving service.*

There are steps then, to attaining Self-Realization. One step includes putting God before anything and everything else. Another step entails being at peace with everyone, because there's no way that we can become one with God without also becoming one, in a sense, with everyone else. We cannot become one with others unless we are at peace with them - loving and forgiving and understanding them.

Our spiritual growth is an issue of free will; we are always free to choose something or someone else besides God to come first in our lives. There is no way to become one with God without putting God first, 100%.

I was delighted to receive confirmation of this message from the Higher Ups, in my devotional reading of <u>Autobiography of a Yogi</u>. Paramahansa Yogananda makes it clear that one has to place God first and foremost in one's goals and above all other desires. Perfectly echoing the messages I have been receiving directly from higher sources (including possibly Paramahansa-ji!), Paramahansa writes that Patanjali warns devotees to seek only God alone, rather than all the wonderful yogic abilities and gifts that come along with becoming one with the Divine, saying that God will only reveal God's Self to those who purely seek God rather than seeking the benefits that God can bestow on us.[44]

---

[43] I know this sounds harsh and counter-cultural to the Prosperity Consciousness of much spirituality in America today. By poverty, I mean letting go of the focus on and desire for material and financial well-being, beyond what one needs to survive and to accomplish one's spiritual mission in life. The essence of spiritual "poverty" is non-attachment to all that is not God, and trusting that God will provide all one's needs while we focus on loving, giving, and serving.

[44] Paramahansa Yogananda, *Autobiography of a Yogi, footnote on p. 266; a beautiful quote – I highly recommend reading it.*

113

May we all be blessed with the pure desire to seek God, and God alone!

The True, Inner Holy Grail

One morning, I asked Jesus Christ in what way he was leading me on the path towards Self-Realization. As I meditated, I had a vision which was not entirely unique to me, as I've seen hints of this in books and read about related concepts, but what was unique was what I was told about this vision, along with the fact that I had just been asking Jesus Christ for a teaching about Self-Realization.

Specifically, I saw a DNA-like pattern, or double helix of energy rising up my spine and lighting up a bowl-shape of light in the top of my head, or crown chakra. What was rather unique to my vision was the DNA-like double-helix of the spiral.

The spiraling energy up the spine has many places been referred to as the serpentine spiritual energy, or Kundalini, rising up the spine. "Kundalini rising" refers to this spiritual energy rising up the etheric spine and energizing the chakras to open them fully, all the way up the spine and to the crown chakra at the top of the head.

This Kundalini awakening helps to take a person to full Self-Realization - eventually, anyway. Sometimes one is neither spiritually nor emotionally prepared for the rising of Kundalini, which can occur through drug use as well as through meditative practices, and, I believe, through tantric sex as well.

When the Kundalini rises up along with spiritual, mental, and emotional preparedness, the Kundalini can fully open the crown chakra

114

for the energetic and spiritual blossoming of the crown chakra (or Sahasrara) into the Thousand-Petaled Lotus. This lotus blossom could also be seen as a "bowl" of light, as in my vision.

As I saw this vision, I was told that this was the true Holy Grail - the inner light which energizes us to be servants of God, and ultimately Self-Realized Masters, if you will. The energy spiraling up the spine forms the stem of the chalice, or grail, while the bowl-shape inside the top of our heads, or crown and brow chakras combined, represents the bowl or cup aspect of the Grail.

Put the vision together with the question asked of Jesus Christ with the announcement that this is the true Holy Grail, and an answer begins to form.

The Inner Holy Grail is the rising of spiritual energies as a person is purified, perfected, and enlightened so that one attains the higher consciousness of one's full brow and crown chakra potential. This full spiritual energy potential is called Self-Realization, in the Hindu tradition. I believe that the Christian tradition would refer to it as perfection. Sanctification, purification, and perfection are the three higher stages of spirituality in Christianity.

I believe Jesus is teaching me that we are meant to achieve true inner communion with God inside ourselves by advancing our spiritual energies, and that this is the true meaning of the Holy Grail.

One of the primary sacraments in Christianity is communion, or Holy Eucharist (or the Lord's Supper, as some Protestants call it.) Yet, the message of this vision seems to be that the true communion of Christ is the inner communion with God through the attainment of Christ-Consciousness, or Perfection. The goal of communion or Holy Eucharist as Christians practice it has been watered down, if you will. The true goal of communion through Jesus Christ is that we will all reach the Christ energy and attain, as Saint Paul put it, "the mind of Christ."

The true Inner Holy Grail is the attainment of Christ energies and Christ-Consciousness within our own selves. How exciting is that - a very real confirmation through my vision that Jesus Christ is indeed calling us to attain Christ-Consciousness - each and every one of us who hear his call and who long for wholeness through following and serving him as Lord and Savior – or as our guru,[45] if you will.

If we are not Christian, or not religious, the call is to become Self-Realized by raising the Kundalini energy up the spine and to attain this highest level of Light-Energy.

No matter what our religion, the True Inner Holy Grail is available to us as we allow our hearts, minds, intentions, words, and actions to be purified, perfected, and enlightened. When our whole being becomes one with the Divine Presence, we experience the rising of the spiritual energies to form the Holy Grail within us.

Nothing could possibly be more holy inside us than to energize the Spirit of God, or Christ-consciousness within our very being.

We are all potentially temples of the Holy Grail.

Legends speak of having to become worthy enough to find the grail, and of having to be purified before one can hold it. These legends carry the essence of truth: the Holy Grail only appears within us when we have attained the pure and holy Christ-energy through devotion and

---

[45] Guru means "spiritual teacher," and from its Sanskrit roots, "dispeller of darkness," which aptly describes the Christ presence, which is also referred to as the "Light of the World." I am indebted to Paramahansa Yogananda's definition on page 3 of *Autobiography of a Yogi*.

service to God.

May the living and loving Light-energy or Christ-energy rise within you as well, that you too, may become the true Holy Grail.

CHAPTER ELEVEN: INCARNATION – EMBODYING DIVINE PRESENCE

In so many ways, I experience the Christ-Consciousness as prompting different attitudes and behaviors toward others, and yes, often to a Christ-like degree that we mere humans don't typically think of as necessary. Of course, I was raised by my mother teaching me and setting that example – at times, anyway.

At age 65, for instance, she traveled to Somalia with Church World Service, in 1993, not long after the U.S. marines had landed there in the midst of violent, turbulent upheaval. She spent six months there, re-opening clinics in villages and re-certifying health workers to give vaccines and so on. Her life was often potentially in danger.

I was raised with not only the teaching, but also the expectation that we live our lives as Christ lived his life, not for ourselves, but for others, and for God. I remember my mother saying, "Life is not about what we get out of life, but about service."

Selfless service is one way of incarnating Divine Presence.

Incarnation is the Christian word for the indwelling presence of the Divine. In Christianity, though, that is usually reserved for Jesus. Beyond this incarnation within Jesus' body, Christianity often denigrates the human body by merely reducing it to a mere vehicle for Divine Presence, or at least, service to the Divine.

Denigration of the body in general in most religions tends to go hand-in-hand with denigration of women's bodies in particular, as well as denial of the Sacred Feminine.

Having been trained in feminist theology at Vanderbilt University Divinity School, I would like to suggest that the concept of incarnation invites a holistic way of understanding Divine Presence that appreciates the body and also affirms the Sacred Feminine.

Although I love the sacredness of the word incarnation, I tend to use the word embodiment or embodying, because this implies a more holistic understanding of the sacredness of both body and spirit, and allows for an expansion of our understandings of embodying the

118

Divine to include pregnancy, childbirth and breastfeeding as sacred ways of "incarnating" the Divine as Unconditional Love.

As the visions and teachings have continued, the general understanding of Self-Realization that I have found myself growing into is the importance of embodying Unconditional Love in all areas of our lives, with all aspects of ourselves. The following teachings reflect this understanding.

Delight!

Do we take delight in one another? When we run into someone we know, do we let them know that we are delighted to see them? Do we let our loved ones know that we are delighted in them each day? Do we work on our own spiritual selves until we take delight even in those with whom we have uncomfortable issues?

That last question reflects some spiritual boot camp work I've been having to face in my morning time of prayer and meditation. We have no need to take delight in people's egos, but we do need to delight in their souls.

Generally, when we think of someone, we think of who they are as a combination of their personality and their egos. Many of us do not often think of people in terms of their souls, except perhaps the really sweet, self-giving, or gentle, soft-spoken people. To delight in others, the way God does, we need to look for people's souls, rather than focusing on the ego-self that each of us tends to show one another on a daily basis.

It helps if we also start living from our higher selves, and interact with others as our higher selves rather than from our own egos as well. To do this, we need to delight in their souls, and we need to delight in our own souls, or higher selves.

Our souls are that piece of God that we bring through to create ourselves at birth. Our higher selves are the part of our souls that are consciously connected with Divine Wisdom, and are fed constantly by Divine Love. All of us have souls, and all of us have Higher Selves. We need to take delight in God's presence within ourselves. Divine presence within each of us consists of our souls, our higher selves, and all those God-given gifts that enable us to be alive and to become the person we are capable of becoming.

When we don't delight in our soul-selves, we are not delighting in God. When we do not delight in others, we are not delighting in God.

One morning, on "Good Morning America," I saw a woman interviewed after disappearing from her family. She commented that she honestly believed that she would not be missed very much. Many of us may have sometimes felt that way, myself included.

Out of having sometimes had that sense of not being very important in other people's lives, I've realized that God must experience that most of the time. I mean, how many of us truly spend any time each day delighting in God? For many of us human beings, God gets a few seconds a day, and if we live a day without reflecting on God, many of us may feel we haven't missed the Divine Presence very much.

Do you ever wonder how frustrated God might feel (if indeed God were to bother with such feelings instead of remaining in perpetual peace and bliss) about the fact that billions of human beings have little or no sense of God's presence, let alone extremely little tendency to delight in who God is?

120

Instead, let's take delight in one another, from one soul to another, and in ourselves, and in God. We are delightful!

ॐ

The Spiritual Artist

When I was a teenager in Africa, I was told that an artist who carves wood is considered to see things in the wood that the rest of us cannot see. Often, statues are carved out of one block of wood. I have been told that a non-artist will say to the artist, "How did you see that in that piece of wood? I did not see it there."

In essence, one carves away all that is not needed, leaving that which one sees as meant to be there. This reminds me of a small table I have which was made in the Congo, with tripod legs carved from one piece of wood, but which fit together like a puzzle. I have never been able to picture how those legs were carved out of that one piece of wood.

It occurred to me that we all need to develop skills as a spiritual artist, carving, not out of wood, but from the interior of ourselves, metaphorically, that is. What we need to 'see' is the presence of God within us. What we need to remove or carve away, is the ego, or lower self.

Learning to see God within ourselves involves removing pride and replacing it with awe and gratitude. Whenever something wonderful happens inside us or through us, we need to realize that it is God acting through us, not ourselves acting.

That is the gift of sight of a spiritual artist. "Blessed are the pure in heart, for they shall see God."

The first step in perceiving this truth is to realize that we have no right to take credit for anything good within ourselves. Being pure in heart means dropping the ego's tendency to take credit. We need to stop seeing ourselves as acting loving or wise in a way that is separate from God.

The second step is rejoicing in being aware that it is God's presence within us - nothing brings greater joy than the recognition that it is God who is being wonderful inside us, rather than thinking that we did something good or talented, or smart or loving.

As someone who is pure in heart, the spiritual artist is also able to see the presence of God in others. We need to delight in the Presence of God as we learn to perceive it in others.

Our canvas, though, is our own lives. We have to learn to paint the presence of God into our lives as we carve out everything inside us that inhibits the presence of God. So, we carve ourselves into a masterpiece of God's presence while also painting the world with the beauty of God's presence. We also reflect the beauty of God's Presence that we see in others. This is the beautiful win-win-win of spiritual artistry.

May you become the spiritual artist God intends for you to be: the blossoming of God's presence into the world through you!

Love Now

Wherever we are, with whomever we find ourselves, we are in the Presence of Love, and we are called to Love. Saints, Bodhisattvas, and Enlightened Ones are called to embody Love, no matter what is going on around them, within them, or to them. Crossing into the land of Christ-Consciousness means holding Divine Love for others as the number one priority of our lives, at all times, in all situations, everywhere we go.

One of the thoughts that I was given to help me with this is:

"This is the time; this is the one."

Meaning, whoever is the person with me at the time, whether total stranger or friend or family member, this is the person whom I am called to love right now.

To shorten the Enlightenment tip:

Love Now.

I think I need to choose that as my personal mantra! More than that, I think I need this as a daily affirmation, a daily meditation, and as a form of prayer without ceasing.

Love Now.

What a lesson we are offered in this lovely thought. Can we practice it? Can we repeat this thought as a constant prayer throughout our day? What doors will be opened if we choose this thought?

Just after I was given this lesson, it happened that a young woman sat down beside me, who appeared to be someone my ego might describe as a 'pretty, but vanilla-flavored, middle-class white American, too young to have had any experiences that would be very interesting.' Do you hear my own ego-based assumptions?

Well, life delightfully got us interacting, and I discovered that she had taught English in France. So, we actually were able to relate *and compare experiences, because I had attended a French private school in West Africa. We discovered that French schools in both France and Africa had two-hour lunches and no organized sports. What fun to have a few moments to connect! So if this young woman was indeed vanilla-flavored, it was more like the custard inside a French éclair!*

When we are in ego-consciousness, we approach people with our automatic judgments and assumptions about them. It is just human nature to do so — that is, our ego-nature to do so. But our human way of seeing them can too often interfere with a more enlightened way of seeing people.

It is helpful to remember that all of us are souls on a human journey, and that our human appearance might not reveal much about our journeys nor our soul-selves. We cannot really understand and know one another until we get to know each other as souls.

Love Now. The person with whom we find ourselves is there for a reason and presents an opportunity for newly embodying Divine Love. We might end up discovering that they are the ones who were called to Be the Presence of Love for us! Of course, the lesson goes both ways, but we don't always see that.

Love Now. Why wait to find out what blessings we might be missing by skipping this lesson? We will be blessed when we choose Love. For Enlightened Ones, choosing Love means holding the other person in that Unconditional Divine Love first and foremost.

May Love guide your vision, and may Love be your path.

ॐ

Left Behind Versus Lifted Up

While I have been substitute teaching in what counts as an urban setting, I have lamented the quality of educational experiences happening for many kids - the ones who, sooner or later, will fall behind, or get left behind. Largely, these individuals are left behind because of economic disadvantages working against them on numerous levels. Essentially, they come from a culture of deprivation: poverty, racism, lack of jobs, and generation-after-generation that have lacked both educational and economic opportunities.

This culture of deprivation seems to lead to a culture of educational depression: both a social and individual lack of interest in education, as well as a lack of excitement and expectation for any sort of positive outcome via education. And so, the cycle repeats.

As a substitute teacher, I have seen children whose families are torn apart by poverty and violence. A middle school boy tells me, "My uncle got shot last night."

A teenage cousin comes into her second grade boy cousin's class after an assembly, and pushes him half way across the coat room. When confronted by me, she, although the elder and supposedly more responsible one, replies "he shoved me first."

Teenagers and children alike whine at me repeatedly. Later, I overheard a mother whining at her daughter in the grocery store, and then I understood why the kids whine - because their mothers whine. Their mothers whine because of way too much stress - more like traumatizing levels of stress - not white collar stress.

Traumatizing stress. I've been there a little bit, for one thing having watched my 34-year-old husband die of a ruptured cerebral aneurysm, and as a single mom, but also later having lived in a state of financial poverty. I've had white collar stress, too, and I can tell you that it is generally nothing like what so many people experience as the combined trauma of poverty and violence.

The stress of poverty, violence, and living in a poor community can lead to utter despair, tons of anger, and a heaping sense of abandonment by society, family, God, and life itself. For many children, these stresses lead to a lack of preparation for school, and either underachievement or failure in school. Essentially, because of poverty, they get left behind.[46]

While, of course, there are many fine schools and fine communities in America, as well as outstanding schools in highly privileged communities, the number one factor undermining many children in America is poverty. Substitute teaching in urban settings can make this readily apparent to those who are willing truly to "see" what is happening in the lives of these children.

Many children in America, and around the world, get left behind.

That phrase recalls for me the popular Christian book series about being "left behind," as well as a religious song I learned as a teenager. Both the book and the song spread the supposed message of Revelation and the gospel of Matthew, the idea that Christ will come again someday, lifting up some people to heaven, and leaving others

---

[46] Yes, I am aware of the "no child left behind" educational policy instituted in the early 2000s here in the United States, and yes, I am saying that, in these cases that I witnessed, it has not yet worked. I am also suggesting that the answers to this problem include not just more "jobs," but also living wages, six months of family leave time for mothers when their children are born, more high-quality subsidized child care, raising taxes on corporations to pay for high-quality public education systems so that, not only will these children succeed in life, but also those corporations can continue to have well-educated, skilled, and success-oriented employees.

behind.

What if the reverse were actually true: instead of seeking to be lifted up ourselves, what if Christ wished for us to lift up others, rather than letting them get left behind — not just spiritually, but emotionally, mentally, and physically?

The Christ of the gospels certainly lived in a way that lifted up people of all socio-economic classes physically (through feeding them and healing them), mentally (through teaching them), emotionally (by treating them well, forgiving them, and calling them by name), and spiritually (by loving them — living and giving his whole life for them).

Do we really dare to believe that Jesus Christ would lift us up if we live our lives in such a way that others are not also lifted up?

If Christ is the one who lifts up, then do we not need to be like him, and lift up others as well?

Lifting up others is what Enlightened Beings do, whether they are called Bodhisattvas, Christs, Yogis, Saints, or Prophets. The only way to have elevated consciousness is to be filled with compassion for others.

May the Holy Presence of the Divine come to you, lifting you up, and lighting the way for you to lift up others as well!

String of Pearls

If you could be part of a string of pearls, which would you prefer to be: one of the pearls, or the string that connects them?

This question came to me from the "Higher Ups" as I was walking the other day. I realized that, while it would be lovely to get to

127

be a pearl and shine in that lustrous, pearly sort of way, far better would it be to be the string which connects the pearls, enabling them to be together, and to show themselves forth to the world.

This choice about being the pearl or the string can be made from either the view of our egos, or from our souls.

Our egos like to be the main event, on center stage, or else they like to hide away, whichever feels more fun or more comfortable at the time. So, our egos might choose to be the pearl, or they might choose to be the string.

Let's notice, though, that the intentions behind choosing to be the string, in the case of the ego that longs to hide, would be self-serving, rather than giving service. Also, the ego's intentions behind choosing to be the pearl are self-aggrandizing.

Our souls and our egos might make the same choices, but for different reasons. Our souls know intuitively, even when our rational minds remain unaware, that our purpose in life is to serve and to show forth Divine Love, until we are all One with Love.

Metaphorically, the pearls may serve and showcase the beauty of Divine Love, but the string also serves Divine Love in a less conspicuous, but more important way. The string unifies; the string unites the individual pearls in a common purpose, for indeed, we are all One.

This unification is the role of Higher Conscious-ness.[47] Enlightened Consciousness unifies our individual purposes into a common goal of love. When we are unified, we can both serve and

---

[47] Again, Higher Consciousness is here used interchangeably with Enlightened Consciousness, Buddha-Consciousness (the Buddha Mind), Unity Consciousness, and Christ-Consciousness.

show forth Divine Love so much more fully and effectively in the world. One pearl is good; a string of pearls is better. Just so, souls united with a loving purpose can bring such greater good into the world.

The world is in great need of receiving more love on all levels - spiritually, energetically, emotionally, mentally, and physically. When we unify our gifts along the string of Christ-Consciousness, we can bring this love through for those who are in need.

Each of us is already a pearl; part of the key to Enlightenment is learning to string our pearls together. May love transform us into both the string, and the pearls, for we are all truly One.

Perfect Love Casts Out Fear

"Beloved, let us love one another, for love is from God: and everyone who loves is born of God and knows God. The one who does not love does not know God, for God is love. We have come to know and have believed the love which God has for us. God is love, and the one who abides in love abides in God, and God abides in him. By this, love is perfected with us, so that we may have confidence in the Day of Judgment; because as He is, so also are we in this world. There is no fear in love; but perfect love casts out fear, because fear involves punishment, and the one who fears is not perfected in love." [48]

The above text from the first letter of John is one of my favorite texts in the Bible. The section I have lifted from the larger passage

---

[48] 1 John 4:7-8, 16-18, *New American Standard Bible*, biblehub.com, copyright 2004-2014 biblos.com

reads like an essential primer for those of us who seek Self-Realization through becoming one with Divine Love. These two simple, yet perfect statements give us much food for contemplation: "God is love" and, "Perfect love casts out fear."

Having felt a lot of fear lately because of the apparent inadequacy of my financial and career situation[49] (truly, to the point of how do I eat, keep a roof over my head, pay all these bills?), this text returned into my consciousness as a teacher, one that I needed to face.

"God is love, and perfect love casts out fear."

The following are the lessons that came to me intuitively from the Higher Ups. Please know that while the lessons below include the term "the devil," one can certainly understand this term as only a metaphor. That is, I invite us to explore the term metaphorically, for whether one believes in a literal devil or does not believe in a devil at all, the term still has metaphorical meanings.

Lesson one:

If God is love, and love casts out fear, then God casts out fear.

If love casts out fear, then fear must be the opposite of love.

If God is love, and love is the opposite of fear, then fear must be the opposite of God.

If fear is the opposite of God, and the devil is the opposite of God, then fear is the devil.

---

[49] I wrote this while substitute teaching, which, again, paid only $65/day (gross pay). I did also have the joy of getting paid a little bit to sing in a church choir!

I cannot stress this teaching enough: "fear is the devil." While writing my second book,[50] praying to be guided directly by Jesus Christ, the intuition came to me: "fear is the only infidel." When we define "infidel" as "unbelieving" and "unfaithful," then fear truly is the only infidel in relation to God as Love. In other words, since fear lacks faith in God, fear is the only thing in the universe that is truly unfaithful to God; fear is the ultimate blasphemy.

Fear is the only infidel.

If God is love, and we are filled with fear, then we are incapable of being one with God, serving God, blessing others, or even having faith in God. Yet, if we are filled with love, we are able to have faith, we are one with God (who is Love), and we are able to serve God as well as to bless and serve others.

Does anything else matter?

Now, I do think it's helpful to think of the 'devil', at least in part, from the perspective of Paramahansa Yogananda, who states that Maya, or the material illusion of this life, is the devil.[51] In this case, then, the devil would be that deceptive state of duality, in which we perceive ourselves as separate from God. This sense of separation from God is what leads us to fear anyway, so yes, the deceptive nature of Maya is one aspect of the devil, the other aspect being fear, which results from the deception of duality.

---

[50] *Exodus 2012: A Mission to Save the Earth.*

[51] Paramahansa Yogananda, *Where There Is Light*, pp. 94, 129.

When contemplating the devil as fear, I had to ask myself if I wanted the "devil" to have so much influence in my consciousness. The obvious answer was 'no'. Of course, obtaining freedom from fear is not always as easy as it sounds, so lessons two, three, and four will follow as we learn to cast out fear. Casting out fear is the way of love. May you walk a path of love today and every day!

Perfect Love Casts Out Fear, Part II

Casting out fear is not easy, especially if you find yourself in a situation in which it literally is hard to survive. Whether we experience health crises such as cancer or other chronic illnesses, or feeling stuck in co-dependent or abusive relationships, or hitting rock bottom financially, or seemingly hopeless depression, or seemingly endless under-unemployment, many of us go through times when we have no idea if or how we are going to get through to the "other side" or maybe even if or how we will survive. While substitute teaching, I did find myself in just such a situation, and I found myself feeling a lot of fear, like a knot wound so tightly in my gut, that it just wouldn't seem to unravel.

Often, when we human beings are in such fearful situations, we might make choices that appear to be 'necessary', and we might call that 'taking responsibility', when another word for it would be, 'acting out of fear'. Often, we make choices more out of fear than out of love. If we feel no fear, we can trust God to lead us and to help us make the choices that will enable our God-given gifts to be used to help other people, while also supporting ourselves and making our dreams come true.

132

I realized that this incredibly challenging point in my life offered both an opportunity to find my true calling in life, and to make choices based on love rather than out of fear. This ultra-challenging situation also forced me to decide whether or not I wanted to live in fear.

Lesson two:

Casting out fear requires the courage to love ourselves unconditionally.

Casting out fear is not easy, but it occurred to me that it takes not so much courage, as it simply requires the courage to love yourself, even when you believe that you have somehow failed utterly, or that God has abandoned you and doesn't love you, or that you must appear utterly unlovable or unrespectable in the eyes of others.

To cast out fear, one has to learn to love oneself unconditionally, and with one's whole self and with one's whole life. This sounds selfish, but ironically, when one can love oneself fully enough to cast fear completely out of oneself, then one becomes far more prepared to love others.

So, since my current life was not working, and even though I really liked many aspects of living in Kalamazoo, I decided to love myself enough to have the courage to work at a new possible direction in my life. I also had the courage to express my integrity by completing a communication I had started as I had previously pursued another possible new direction in life.

These were my first attempts at finding connections for moving to the Washington, DC, area. In the first case, I felt hope, although there were certainly no guarantees that this direction would work out. In

133

the second case, I felt a sense of peace that I was probably closing a door, though with integrity and respect. In both cases, at least one door seemed to crack open before the end of that same day.

Love leads to faith, and together, love and faith not only cast out fear, but also open doors. Experiencing both faith and love within ourselves leads to joy. May you love yourself so much, that no one else can take that joy away from you!

Perfect Love Casts Out Fear, Part III

Have you ever found yourself in such a prolonged and difficult situation, that fear becomes an old, bad habit?

Lesson three:

If fear has taken up residence within you, laugh at it, because it is a bad habit that is only an illusion.

If you're struggling to let go of fear, laugh at it and tell fear that it is nothing more than a bad habit! Laughing in the face of fear is one sure-fire way to achieve victory over it. So, why not love yourself enough to laugh - a little or a lot?

Go ahead, laugh at fear, as though it is this foolish person standing before you taunting you (again, the devil, metaphorically speaking). Laugh at fear, and literally tell it that it is nothing but an old bad habit and, like a pair of old shoes, while it may seem familiarly comfortable, it is time for it to go. Why not also laugh at yourself, because you can see how silly it is that you have been holding onto something painful.

It may not be easy to laugh at ourselves, and you may object that you find yourself in a serious situation, but that is just fear speaking, or thinking, again. This is when it is helpful to remember that whatever situation we find ourselves in, it is just Maya, or illusion – only real enough for us to learn a few lessons from it and move on.

This is a lesson from Buddha; it helps us to take ourselves less seriously, and hopefully at some point reach that attainment of "no-self." This could be called Buddha-therapy: seeing the unwholesomeness of ego and laughing at it until we release it, and let go into the space of no-self – that emptiness, where the still, small voice of our Higher Selves awaits to be heard, felt, discovered.

The true inner Self has no fear, because it remains non-attached to all but that state of love, peace, bliss – Nirvana, or ecstasy, or Samadhi.

Remembering gratitude, remembering to choose some loving affirmations, we may then laugh, be grateful, affirm a more gracious and loving reality, and move on. This is the loving thing to do. May Love cast all fear from you and your life.

Perfect Love Casts Out Fear, Part IV: The Tao

The final lesson I was learning about casting out fear is, I believe, the most difficult of all: non-attachment.

Please allow me to explain how I was led to the realization of this spiritual truth. One morning, I felt led to read a book of parallel *sayings of Jesus Christ and Lao Tzu, which had been given to me some time ago.[52] All I had done was peruse it.*

As I was reading about who Lao Tzu had been, and the story of his writing of the Tao Te Ching, I realized that I was once again, for the first time in a long time, hearing 'The Teacher Voice' in my head. Furthermore, I realized that The Teacher Voice is not always the voice of an Enlightened Master, but sometimes the Voice of the Tao, or the Voice of Wisdom which Enlightened Masters hear.

Eureka! Oh, what joy to hear again the Teacher Voice! I realized at once two things: first, that I must hold no attachment to anything, including having 'enough' money, and including having a roof over my head. Second, I realized that the Teacher Voice was telling me that staying calmly in the Presence through all situations in life is the pearl of great price, and if we have found the pearl, nothing else matters in life.

Jesus used the expression 'the pearl of great price' as one way to explain the kingdom of God. Certainly, if we are letting God, or Divine Love, reign through us, then we are staying calmly in the Presence.[53]

To get there, however, we have to have a purity of heart and intention in which we let go of all things, let go of all people, let go of all expectations, hopes, and dreams, and just live in the peace and love of that Inner Presence.

---

[52] This was a Christmas gift from my daughter-in-law, before she became my daughter-in-law (which I'm so glad she did).

[53] Matthew 13:45-46: "Again, the kingdom of heaven is like unto a merchant man, seeking goodly pearls: Who, when he had found one pearl of great price, went and sold all that he had, and bought it." King James Version

Lesson Seven:

Casting out fear requires letting go of all earthly attachments.

So, even when we are living in life-threatening situations, whether due to danger, or illness, or finances, or what-have-you, we can live in peace, joy, and love. By letting go of attachment, we can achieve inner peace and serenity. In fact, non-attachment is the only avenue to this inner serenity. This is a primary tenet of Buddhism.

When we trust the Oneness of ourselves and Divine Love with all that is, non-attachment allows us to be part of the flow of Life in the most positive sense, not necessarily either receiving or not receiving what we need or want, but just being one with the flow of what is needed — both giving and receiving.

Christians have the beautiful phrase: "the peace of God, which transcends all our powers of thought, will be a garrison to guard your hearts and minds in Christ."[54] *Notice, when we mention Christ — we are speaking of that consciousness of unity with all being.*

In every moment of distress, we need to look honestly at what we are holding onto, and Let Go! We are free to have preferences, but we need hopefully and lovingly to express our preferences to God and then Let Go and trust Love to do what's best.

Next, we also need to let Love do what's best through us. We need to commit our hearts to hold only loving intentions, our minds to

---

[54] Philippians 4:7, Weymouth New Testament. While the text actually says, "in Christ Jesus," we are here referring to the higher perspective, understanding that Jesus set the example, but that all of us can attain this Christ-Consciousness, by the grace of God.

hold only loving hopes, our hands only to do works of Love, our voices to speak only words of Love, and our feet to follow only in paths of loving-kindness.

If we do this in every moment, fear will have no foothold, because its tentacles consist of that ugly thing called attachment.

The Tao, or the Way, is the Way of Non-Attachment, a Zen-like peaceful acceptance of all things. Only out of this place of peace can we live a life without fear, and filled with love.

It seems impersonal, and it is impersonal, because to hold onto our personhood is also a form of attachment.

The Tao:
Casting out fear
and remaining in
the peace of Divine Love
is the Tao, or the Way.
Casting out fear and Being Love
is the way, the truth, and the life.
May you discover the radiant joy of living without fear,
the peace and bliss of Tao, the Way of Life!

CHAPTER TWELVE: TRANSITION ON ALL LEVELS: MOVING TO WASHINGTON, DC

I believe it was in January or February of 2011 when I realized that where I wanted to live was really the Washington, DC, area. Because my dad was from Ohio and my mom was from Texas, and because my life growing up had included living in three different countries in Africa and three different states in the United States, and because we had generally moved every year or two, I became a "global nomad," a person without a home community.

While growing up, the only place I had ever had time to begin to feel at home was in Chevy Chase, Maryland, a suburb of Washington, DC,[55] where we had lived for six whole years in a row. My parents had sold their house there while I was in college, so there was no obvious way to go back "home." I had longed to return there ever since, and in fact, during college, had managed to spend one semester as an intern in DC.

Finally, I truly decided to follow my former healing client's advice, and "put myself out there," contacting yoga centers in and around DC to see if there was any possibility of working there. I really only contacted two at that time. The first was the owner of a yoga studio that had existed in the luxury of the DuPont Circle area. For some reason, he had moved it, and had bought a row house in Anacostia, an area of DC isolated across the Anacostia River, with high crime rates and a lot of extreme poverty. He was open to my coming down to meet him, potentially to stay in the house, to help him re-start the yoga center there in Anacostia.

The other was a yoga studio in Reston, Virginia, where there

---

[55] I find it humorous but understandable that Americans who live far away from Washington, DC refer to it as "Washington," which of course can be confused with the State of Washington, whereas people who live in or near Washington, DC simply call it "DC" or refer to something as "in the district." I personally enjoy referring to Washington, DC as simply, "DC."

were rooms for doing energy healing work, or Reiki. The woman with whom I spoke was open to meeting with me.

Realistically, I could not see how any of this was going to happen, so I probably dragged my feet. The end of the school year came. I no longer had a job, no income, and the only thing that seemed to make sense was to go down to DC to look for a job. Yet, I still felt hesitant.

So, I prayed to Paramahansa Yogananda: "Paramahansa-ji, please help me open your book (*Autobiography of a Yogi*) to the story which will help me decide whether or not to go to Washington, DC."

I opened the book to the story in which Paramahansa-ji's older brother sends the young Paramahansa and a friend on a one-way train ticket to a holy city, telling Paramahansa that if he gets everything paid for plus the gift of a return ticket, he would become Paramahansa's disciple that same night. Well, everything worked out more than beautifully for Paramahansa and his friend, so I decided that a one-way ticket to Washington, DC, was okay for me!

Since my daughter already lived in Washington, DC, I went down and stayed with her for about ten days, applying for jobs with non-profit organizations. I had two interviews for starter jobs, doing street fundraising. I had previously done door-to-door community organizing for renewable energy in Michigan, so I knew that I could qualify for such a position.

The more professional jobs in the DC area are all highly competitive, with seemingly unlimited candidates with perfect credentials, compared with my diverse, and mostly church-related background. No church openings had been available to me.

I went to the Reston yoga studio, and because of some misunderstanding on my part about when to arrive, that meeting did not go as well as I might have hoped. I believe I also met the owner of the yoga house in Anacostia, and he invited me to stay for free at the house and to promote meditation classes there in order to help re-awaken his dream.

I also contacted Dr. Victoria Goldsten, HD, Homeopathic

Doctor and Director of the Washington Institute of Natural Medicine, and met with her about becoming an energy healer and life coach at the Institute. Dr. Goldsten graciously welcomed me to be a practitioner at the Washington Institute. Progress!

After making these connections, I returned to Michigan, where some friends and neighbors helped me put everything in storage. One friend took in my cat, Picasso.[56] Unfortunately, my dog Comet, who at age 14, had been ailing and in pain for over a year, developed seizures right before I needed to leave. My neighbors lovingly advised me to "put her down," because there was literally no way I could risk driving on the Pennsylvania turnpike with my dog having seizures in the car.

I also had no money to speak of, so I had to take Comet to the vet, paid for by one of my loving neighbors, and have her put to sleep. Aside from God, Comet had been the most loving and long-standing companion of my life.

Next, kind friends helped me put all of my furniture and boxes of "stuff" in storage – there can be a lot of "stuff" when you're 52 and you've raised two children. Then we loaded my car, including filling a roof-top carrier that one friend lent to me.

The night after we loaded up my car to the gills, I went online and found out that I had been accepted for one of the street fundraising jobs. So, I could drive to DC with a sense of peace, not just the peace of faith, but also with tangible reassurance that God indeed was watching out for me.

One friend and a different neighbor handed me cash, totaling $250, which enabled me to buy gas and pay tolls driving to DC. It also enabled me to eat until I could get my first, small paycheck.

I was emotionally and spiritually buoyed by the fact that the Universe had provided me a "home" and a job and a place to begin to do energy healing. Although all three aspects of my life came with

---

[56] This friend had a residential home for adults with mental disabilities. Picasso eventually made himself quite at home, becoming a blessing to everyone there. He seemed to find his calling, as though he has become a Yogi cat!

enormous challenges, it was overall a beautifully wondrous shift in my life, *and* I got to live in Washington, DC!

For the next thirteen months, I worked full-time "street fundraising" for children's charities, seeking to get people to sign-up to sponsor a child somewhere in the world. I also began seeing clients at the Washington Institute of Natural Medicine, and finished writing my second book, *Exodus 2012: A Mission to Save the Earth,* which I self-published in July of 2012.

In *Exodus 2012,* my intention was to bring through, prayerfully guided by Jesus, what his message would be if he came back today. However, in the story, I had Jesus return, not in the way Christians expect, but reincarnated as a Chinese Tai Chi master, with a mission to save the earth from climate change. For me, the amazing experience of writing the book was that of being intuitively guided, so that I actually experienced in my own head what it is like for a master to dialogue with people, often turning their own arguments around on them with a series of questions, like the true master that Jesus is!

As soon as I could find a couple of part-time professional jobs to replace street fundraising, I quit, because it was really hard on my aging body. One part-time job I began was serving a traditional church three days a week. The other part-time job was temporarily promoting attendance of Disciples of Christ at an activist conference that advocates with Congress on a variety of justice issues. I continued to see clients at the Institute.

December 2012

This book would be remiss if I did not share spiritual shifts that occurred in me and in my life during December 2012, and yes, even on December 21, 2012, the last day of the Mayan Calendar. I will share two experiences here, and in the chapter on Consciousness, I will share what I learned, which I call "Lessons from Above."

Many spiritual people have recognized this date as a day of shifting energies, for the earth, for people on earth, and perhaps for the entire cosmos. I will leave those suppositions to others, although I have read interesting commentaries on the subject.

What I experienced were two primary events in myself, as well as ever-expanding abilities and experiences during my sessions with clients, whether energy healing or life-coaching.

One of the primary events happened on the day of December 21st itself. While I was meditating, I asked about ascension, because there were spiritual predictions that this would be a time of ascension for many.

I experienced myself ascending through my crown chakra, as I have before, and was told that I could now ascend anytime I desired. In other words, by intention and focus, I could ascend to higher realms, including my favorite "Land of Foggy White Light." This is indeed what I have experienced since then, unusual though it may sound to ascend to higher realms through one's crown chakra – perhaps it is through the brow chakra, or a combination of both; I just know I "go up."

The other experience was just as dramatic and more far-reaching in a practical sense of touching the lives of others. I was giving energy healing to a client whom I had seen several times before, and who gave me permission to share her name in this book. Helena Falla is a delightful soul, a fun client, and a beautiful and intelligent woman.

As I was being a vessel for healing energy to flow into Helena through her head, I was told that Helena holds the intention of bringing out the truth so strongly, that I could initiate her as a light worker.

Then it came to me how to initiate her as a light worker, blessing her with the Seven Archangels of the Seven Rays.

Then it came to me that I could teach light worker training.

Now, please understand that, until this point, "light worker" was not a term I used often, thought about much, or considered as essential terminology on the spiritual path. I had been told I was a light worker, by someone who would clearly know, but that was about it.

When the healing energy portion of the session with Helena was done, I told her what had come to me, and offered her the initiation and blessing of the Archangels. Helena seemed to feel so blessed, and I felt so moved, that I began to develop "Light Worker Training," and began to teach my first class in January 2013.

Helena did not take the class until the fall of 2013, but when it came time for the initiations, she had appreciated it so much the first time, that she asked for the initiation blessing again!

Light Worker Training is now something I offer somewhat regularly, and have developed a level two for people who would like to do energy healing. I also plan to develop a level three for people who would like to learn to coach others intuitively. I love this work! Of course, I also love doing energy healings and intuitive life coaching!

In the meantime, I did not necessarily expect the church position, which was a clergy position, to last very long, given the history of ministers and members having already left the church, although one does hope for the best. After supply-preaching there for a couple of months, I went to the church because I needed a part time job, and because they needed help.

My heart went out to the members and leaders of the church, and I went simply with the intention of helping the church members learn some techniques for growing churches. Of course I grew fond of the people, and desired to stay in order to serve with and for them, but my main goal was to help them learn how to grow a church.

While attendance in worship about doubled while I was preaching there, my efforts at teaching the church members techniques that they could use to grow the church did not succeed. The aspect of serving churches that I always struggled with the most was the politics; this situation was no exception. I left in July of 2013.

For a long time, I had understood why church politics seemed so difficult for me both from the perspective of family systems theory and also in terms of my own spiritual values and emotional processes. However, it was not until April 2015, that I met an older healer who finally helped me make sense of the challenges I had faced in churches, which are, like families, virtually always dysfunctional systems to some extent.

First, I brought in past life karmic energies of being a prophet or at least of resistance to religious authorities, and second, as an empath and energy healer, I am not only extremely sensitive to feeling energies of individuals and groups, but also I have tended to absorb rather than shield myself from the painful energies of others.

This sensitivity to the energetic level of the dysfunction has always increased both my spiritual objections to the dynamics of groups and my emotional vulnerability to them because of sensing not just my own emotional pain in the group, but also the emotional pain, often subconscious, of everyone else in the group. I usually confronted the dysfunctional systems like a prophet (apparently an old pattern), because I could feel how out of alignment they were with Divine energies of love and peace.

This probably did not help anyone in most cases, except perhaps the few who felt released from the dysfunctional systems along with me. Because of my unhappiness with dysfunctional patterns in churches, my dream has long been to start a spiritual community that functions harmoniously. I believe this can be accomplished by focusing on everyone's personal responsibility, much like 12-Step programs, because this is the only way to minimize dysfunction, along with striving to embody higher energies of Divine Love and peace ourselves, instead of relying on an external "savior" to create harmony for us.

When I quit the church job in July 2013, I had no other job besides seeing clients – primarily at the Washington Institute of Natural Medicine, and I did not have adequate marketing skills nor any budget with which to promote my work well, despite the fact that, by that time, I was living in rented rooms which included one large and energetically beautiful "healing and meditation room" where I could see clients.[57] Again, I found myself in a precarious financial situation. However, I also found that the weeks when I had more faith, more clients and more income appeared.

Otherwise, I had plenty of time for meditation and spiritual reflection, especially in the fall of 2013, after my son's wedding in August.

The summer of 2013 began the period of "mornings with the Masters." I have never been much of a morning person, at least not since I was about 7 or 8 years old, but although I did not begin my days especially early, I did generally dedicate a long time, after my morning walk, to yoga-like stretches and then a long time of prayer and meditation.

I am just now beginning to shift to the meditation happening early, before my morning walk. The Ascended Masters, angels, and Archangels are available 24/7, but our human degree of attunement with them and with the Divine may vary in direct proportion with our distractions – until we become Self-Realized and stable in the bliss-

---

[57] The story of my housing situation for the first year-and-a-half I was in the DC area included many challenges, but God always provided through helpful other people. Plus, one landlady became one of my best clients for giving energy healing to her various species of pets – what fun! – and another landlady became the source of distance healing "clients," whose responses to distance healing count among the most amazing miracles I have experienced in my work.

peace-love of Nirbikalpa Samadhi, that is!

So, beginning earlier is better, and spending long times in meditation is central to our spiritual development, intuition, attunement, and ability to heal, teach, and guide others.

I believe that Raja Yoga meditation and Kriya Yoga meditation, faithfully practiced, constitute our best investment of time on the spiritual path. Of course, no spiritual practices are especially worthwhile if we do not hold high and pure intentions.

While I did look for a "job," I found that the competition in this area around Washington, DC is really steep, especially for those of us over 50 who haven't specialized in an area enough to become an "expert." I applied for two church ministerial positions, and was not accepted for either of them. One of the churches literally rejected me because I do energy healing, saying that the older members with whom I would be working would not understand it. I decided no longer to seek to serve a traditional church, though I dearly love so many aspects of serving churches.

When serving traditional churches, whether conservative or liberal in their beliefs, one still has to teach and preach from a traditional Christian paradigm. Serving churches always meant that I could not talk about reincarnation, nor about all of us being invited to attain Christ-Consciousness, nor about the path of Self-Realization, and so on. When it got to the point of not being able to do energy healing, it became too much.

So, after three or four months looking for a job, I stopped. Instead, I spent my time meditating and seeking to connect with God and the Ascended Masters more and more. This is what I felt led to do.

I thank God for these morning lessons that I learned with the Masters.

147

CHAPTER THIRTEEN: INTERLUDE OF MIRACLES

In July of 2013, I heard Jesus say to me,
"Let go the 'I.'"

The Ascended Masters clearly said to me:
"There is no 'me;' there is only 'us.'"

August 2013

Although we know that for our progress on the spiritual path, it becomes essential to focus on God rather than seeking any special God-given "powers," and while I have no desire to seek powers other than to allow God, through me, to help people and animals heal physically, emotionally, and spiritually, nonetheless amazing miracles did sometimes occur in this period of my life.

I hesitate to write about them, because this story is primarily about the teachings and other benefits the Ascended Masters can bring to our lives and the lives of others as we learn to how to connect with them. To me, the Ascended Masters and their teachings are the focal point of attention, but clearly, the healings are another benefit, as many great souls throughout history have also been known for healing.

In fact, I sense the Divine Mother/Father inviting me to share a few stories so that you can see that, while we seek to grow closer to God, God then uses us to help others. After all, the intention of growing closer to God can only come true if we also hold the intention of serving and blessing others, because that is Who God Is and what God does: God blesses people (and animals!).

Also, this sharing may serve as a partial answer to the question that may be in some readers' minds: "are there any practical benefits to pursuing this spiritual path?" to which one might answer, "of course, but the practical benefits cannot be the focus as we seek to become one with God."

At any rate, I hesitate to call attention to myself and my life positively except to say that God deserves the credit for everything positive in myself and my life. However, people sometimes misinterpret such sharing as calling attention to oneself, or as bragging. For the sake of showing the wondrous nature of Divine Presence in our lives, please allow me to share how amazingly God can help people through us when we dedicate ourselves to becoming one with God and blessing others.

The occasion was the weekend of my son's wedding in Massachusetts. He and his wife, both graduates of St. John's College in Annapolis, Maryland (the "Great Books School"), are beautiful, highly intelligent souls with a wonderful circle of friends and family. At the time, they lived in Cambridge, and got married on her aunt and uncle's farm, just one mile from Walden Pond. What a delightful combination of nature, romance, and karmic blessings!

That weekend, I stayed with some good friends who live in Holden, Massachusetts. They were my best neighbors (ever!) when we all lived in Kalamazoo, Michigan.

Before leaving home, I had already received the intuition that my mother, who was ailing and who had some form of dementia, would be unable to make it to the wedding, so I was planning on visiting her in New York after the wedding weekend.

Sure enough, while my son and I were in a store shopping for an item for the rehearsal dinner,[58] my sister called, sounding quite distressed, and saying that our mother was too sick to come to the wedding – her blood pressure had just shot up sky-high, she had a

---

[58] I do feel sad to say that I was too broke to help him purchase even a $20 item. My contributions to the wedding included two large and very expensive homemade cheesecakes (a specialty I learned in this life), and 9 feet of hand-crocheted bunting which decorated their table at the wedding reception. I love to crochet lacy items, although this is one of many material blessings I have had to let go of most of the time on this spiritual path.

terrible headache, and she had not even gotten out of bed.

My sister is a nurse, and generally handles these things calmly and rationally. She kind of wanted our mom to come to the wedding, but she insisted that if Mom died at the wedding, she would not resuscitate her. I also sensed how much my mom wanted to come the wedding (she had actually remembered that it was happening), but my son had no desire for his grandmother to die at their wedding, understandably so. (My mom would have wanted everyone to keep celebrating anyway, because to her, death meant getting to celebrate being in heaven with Jesus.)

So, I reassured my sister, "Don't worry, I'll pray for her now, and I will send distance healing to her later. You need to plan to come to the wedding and not feel guilty." I wanted to reassure my sister that mom would be fine, because I trusted the distance healing process and sensed she would be fine, but one can never guarantee anything, of course.

I prayed for Mom then, and spoke with my sister later that day, only to find out that Mom had gotten out of bed, got dressed, and got in her wheelchair to be taken to get medication for her headache.

That night, I sent distance healing to her, asking for her blood pressure to come down. When I send distance healing, I ask for the Seven Archangels of the Seven Rays to bring through the healing energy, just as I do with in-person healings, so they are actually doing the healing; I am just showing up and praying and serving as a vessel for the intention of healing.

Over the course of the wedding weekend, a friend who had experienced some dramatic distance healing for her cousin having happened through me, contacted me for another healing. She texted me to ask if I would send distance healing to a friend of hers whose appendix had burst, and whose blood pressure was too low for them to operate on her.

All I need for distance healing is the person's permission or a relative's permission, and the person's name (Technically, not even that much is necessary, but that is my preference and honors everyone's free will). I prefer also seeing a picture of them, so that I can "see" them as I send healing.

My friend texted a picture, so the same weekend that I was praying for my mother's blood pressure to come down to save her life, I also got to pray and send healing for another woman's blood pressure to come up, so the doctors could do surgery and save her life.

Now, it was late at night after a day of wedding celebrations when I got to send the distance healing to this friend of a friend. After I started sending the energy, I could "see" that she was out-of-body. The sense that I got was that she did not want to be in her body because it was too painful. So her soul was hovering, like a golden glow, above her body.

She had a choice to make. I knew that I needed to "talk" with her about this choice, because I had, years before, "called" a woman out of a coma and back into her body by "talking" with her soul-to-soul about making a choice while she was in a coma. I had also long before "called" a friend's mother back into her body when she was having an out-of-body experience in the hospital, and semi-consciously writhing about and refusing all treatment, food, and fluids. Each time, one has to make it clear to the person's soul that they have a choice to make, or their body will die.[59]

So, I told my friend's friend that she had a choice to make, but that her friends and family were not ready to lose her, and that she could choose to come back into her body to love them if she wanted to. All of a sudden, I saw a big golden glow in her heart chakra, and I knew that she had chosen to come back into her body.

I felt elated, though extremely tired. I really had to trust the Archangels for help sending the healing, because I felt so exhausted, I

---

[59] I am aware of the dramatic sound of these "claims." The woman whom I called back into her body from a coma had been a church member in a church I had served many years before. When she came out of the coma, she was unable to speak, but when she saw me, she grinned with absolute joy. My training in England had taught us that it is possible to communicate with others, soul-to-soul.

152

was nearly falling asleep. So, I began to "send" the healing energy (provided by God and the Archangels, of course.) While I was sending, I saw and sensed the Archangels sucking the pain, the inflammation, and – yes – the infection out of the woman's appendix. I was so surprised by the sense that they were able to suck out infection that I literally looked up and asked out loud, "You can do that?"

After the Archangels sucked out the pain, inflammation, and infection, I sent white light in to fill her whole abdomen, in case there were any stray bits of infection spread out anywhere, and finished sending energy healing to her in general.

The next day, I heard from my friend that the woman's blood pressure had risen enough for them to do surgery, so would I send distance healing again. It ended up that I sent distance healing to the woman whose appendix had ruptured a total of three times in about three days, while I was still away from home.

I had also been sending distance healing to my mom, whose blood pressure had come down enough for her to get out of bed and go in her wheelchair to receive medication for her headache, almost immediately after I had prayed.

So, this one weekend, I had been sending distance healing to one woman for her blood pressure to come down, and to another woman for her blood pressure to come up, and in both cases, God and the Archangels came through and delivered what was needed!

When I left Massachusetts, I headed to the nursing home in New York, where I had visited my mother once before. I was greeted by the Activities Director, a very friendly older woman with whom I had gotten acquainted during my previous visit.

She greeted me: "Your mother is so much better! Her blood pressure went down! And look, the swelling in her legs has gone down!"

I responded (simply, because I "knew"): "I know; I sent her distance healing.

"You did?!" The woman asked.

"Yes, I replied. "Do you remember last fall when mom was in

153

the hospital, and I came up to be with her, and she got out of the hospital 24 hours later?"

"Yes."

"I gave her energy healing in the hospital."

"You did?!" She asked, surprised again.

"Yes. Do you remember last spring when I visited, and brought my mom to the dining room for breakfast with her walker, and you all said, "Joy, where's your wheelchair?"

"Yes." (I had no idea that my mom had been using the wheelchair. The morning after I had given her a healing, she just got up and reached for her walker instead!)

"I had given her energy healing then, too."

"You did?!"

My mom had seemingly always responded well physically to the healing work I did with her, but it had never seemed to significantly help her dementia (although who knows, it might have slowed its progression).

We had a lovely visit, and then I returned home, having had to delay teaching a meditation class as I had anticipated, and had told the students ahead of the wedding that I might have to delay it to visit my mom.

I have no idea how knowing things ahead of time works. I have no idea how distance healing works. I have no rational explanation for how in-person healing "works." I just know that it often noticeably benefits, and always works on some level. The Universe is an amazing, wonderful, and beautiful place to me!

As if to confirm this reality, when I got home, my friend told me that her friend had had her surgery to remove her appendix. When the doctors opened her up, there was no infection! (I guess the Archangels are in fact able to remove infection, after all!) Her friend has fully recovered and is doing well.

ॐ

CHAPTER FOURTEEN: MORNINGS WITH THE MASTERS

Fall 2013

Buddha Teaches Me Daily Non-attachment

During the fall of 2013, I found myself in the situation of seeking to make a living solely by seeing clients and occasionally teaching meditation or light worker training to a student or two. What a challenge it was to get through the end of the year financially.

At some point, I began to eat less. I would eat half of a meal, and save the other half, knowing that at least I would have something to eat the next day.

This practice actually developed into a spiritual practice. Buddha started working with me to get me to be less attached to those things that we tend to take for granted.

I had long ago given up coffee for tea. I had also long ago given up eating meat. I had been single and celibate much of my life, even though I had always desired to remarry. I had imbibed very little alcohol for the previous few years, in part as a spiritual discipline, and in part because it turned out that the scleritis in my eye flared up whenever I ate sugar or drank wine. Because of the scleritis, I obviously had to give up eating sugary foods on a regular basis as well.

Who knew that a condition like scleritis could be a spiritual task master! However, like a red signal flag to let me know when I was spiritually out of sorts, it had even flared up when I went felt fear and stress. So, that horrible condition served spiritual purposes very well!

Now, I also knew that I needed to give up watching movies and TV series on Netflix – or at least seriously reduce watching Netflix. Apparently, that has been my "go-to" for de-stressing and for tuning out from life for a while. I began to be aware of watching Netflix as a somewhat of an addiction. Not the kind of addiction where it takes over your whole life, but just that there were times when I would start watching it, and not be able to stop myself in time to go to bed before midnight.

I did not feel prepared to give it up. In fact, I still let myself watch it once a week or so, although I believe I have now learned that I don't "need" it, and that I desire it less and less, because watching the shows generally lowers my consciousness down to a more material plane.

But Buddha was working with me. I sensed him wanting me to give up eggs, over which I hesitated as well, not that I typically eat many on an ongoing basis. I sensed him wanting me to give up caffeinated tea, so I began to reduce my caffeinated tea intake, in part by switching to hot water with freshly squeezed lemon juice and freshly minced ginger, which is actually a delightful and very healthy combination. I gave up caffeinated tea the week of Christmas, 2013. (I did later return to drinking just one cup or mug a day, although I can now also go without caffeinated tea when I choose to do so.)

I sensed Buddha asking me to eat less, even when I had the financial means to eat a full meal. Clearly, Buddha was working with me to practice non-attachment on some very practical levels, and quite daily as well. I think I did some juice fasting as well (fasting is not my favorite spiritual discipline!).

The spiritual path is an everyday journey, apparently. This *every* day quality of maintaining higher consciousness through spiritual disciplines can seem to make the challenging aspects even more challenging, because there seem to be no vacations from higher consciousness, without a lot of anguish, that is!

October 21, 2013

While walking on a beautiful fall day, I heard:

156

This is the beginning of lessons on Mastery.
Let go the "I."
Let go of the desire for "I."
Perceive the unity in all things. It is not enough to know "I
AM;" for "We Are."

From my time of meditation I heard:

Just as the Infinite is split into many forms, so, too, the reverse
is true. The many forms dissolve into the Infinite. This is the true
Essence of Form: We Are One.

Let the Energy of Unity, which is the Aum, which is Bliss,
energize your form, so that you perceive beyond Illusion, the Unity of
Form.

10-25-13

As I was struggling with hope that one of my heart's dreams
would come true in the face of circumstances that suggested otherwise,
I heard Buddha ask me:

"Why are you so attached to this little lifetime?"

10-26-13

When I meditated, I reflected on this question: "why are you

157

so attached to this little lifetime?"

All of a sudden, I could see the vast vistas of infinity – time and space unlimited by my human form and this human life. When we remain attached to the outcomes of this life, we limit ourselves and who we are. If we feel attached to certain events and relationships turning out certain ways, we limit the power of the Infinite to be born within us.

10-28-13

This is what I heard from The Teacher Voice:

There are three forms of manifestation of spirit (the Unborn) in humanity: the physical, the mental/intellect, and the emotional. To birth the unborn, one must manifest each aspect with non-attachment, because the Unborn is beyond mere manifestation and therefore always remains unattached. What is birthed in each aspect is love, wisdom, and the energy of life expressing itself in forms of beauty. But only fully birthed through non-attachments, because that's what Unborn means, in part: "Beyond attachment" or Infinity.

You have heard it said, and perhaps seen it written, that "The fear of the Lord is the beginning of wisdom," but I say to you, humility is the beginning of wisdom.

Humility is the expression of non-attachment to the intellect.

God has to give free will, because God is the Uncreated Infinite, and therefore is non-attached with regard to the manifested forms of the Universe.

Liberty and Love go together because granting others the liberty to be themselves, to act and think and speak as themselves, is the act of

158

loving with non-attachment, which is the way God loves.

As I am compiling these lessons in the spring of 2015, I realize that this non-attached quality, combined with love-peace-bliss, is the state of Being which may be called the Tao. It is from this state of Being that God creates, and it is from this state of Being that we also are able to create or manifest with God-like effects.

This is what I experience during energy healing – a state that may be called the Tao. Today, I have been re-initiated in this Tao. What a great place to be!

Here follows a series that is part of a larger series which I was told, by the Ascended Masters with whom I work, are *"Lessons in Mastery."*

This smaller series I am calling *"The I Am Diaries."*

One morning, the importance of returning to the "I AM" teachings of Saint Germain as expressed in "The I Am Discourses"[60] became crystal clear to me. I had been struggling with at least two significant issues in life, and knew that a return to "I AM" consciousness was the ticket to returning to higher consciousness and a more fulfilling life.

One of the central concepts in "The I Am Discourses" is that "the mighty presence of God" is the only active presence in this world.[61] Another central concept is that we can either look to the outer world of form to seek fulfillment, which will be temporary and illusory, or we can turn to the inner manifestation of divine Presence and find

[60] Ascended Master Saint Germain, *The "I AM" Discourses,* (Chicago: Saint Germain Press), Godfré Ray King and Lotus Ray King, Editors, 1936.
[61] Ibid, pp. 2-3.

fulfillment which is permanent.[62] The Presence of God within us is what is productive of positive, loving, perfecting, and prosperous results in the outer manifestations of life.

Because of the beauty of these teachings, I embarked once again on living from the consciousness of I AM "the mighty presence of God …in action. … I AM the great opulence of God made visible in my use right now and continuously."[63] (Thank you for those affirmations, Saint Germain!)

At the same time, I held the intention of turning first and foremost to my experience of Divine Presence within me for satisfaction, nurturing, fulfillment, and love, rather than seeking it outside myself.

While I strayed from that intention from time to time, largely, my sense of self as well as my experience of life improved remarkably.

Please note that these lessons in Self-Realization kept including the instruction not to seek a 'job' as a means of support. Rather, I felt led to trust Divine Providence through the energy healing and life coaching work that I do. What a challenge this has felt like to the part of me that "just wants a job with benefits, because then I wouldn't have to worry about money anymore"! Our culture's view of the all-importance of getting, having, and keeping a job now seem to me to constitute an overwhelmingly strong form of idolatry in which the priority of having a job becomes our god.[64]

Well, now the latter is one way of experiencing consciousness about my 'reality.' I believe most people would view it that way: "just get a job!" In Spirit, I felt led to believe and to trust that all will be well as I pursue my life's callings, and as I work hard to make my God-given dreams come true, as these dreams benefit others.

---

[62] Ibid, p. 16.

[63] Ibid, pp. 13 and 18.

[64] Please understand that having a job and working hard constitute two different realities in my mind. I believe in the importance of hard work at most points along the spiritual path. However, I invite us to develop a spiritual attitude toward work.

One morning, I felt a shift within myself as I was meditating, and the affirmation came to me: "I am the beauty that is within me." In other words, I am God's beauty that is inside me – there's no separation between me and God.

In the context of having felt tons of self-doubt for years and years, as well as knowing that I have God-given gifts that have seemed mostly overlooked in the outer world, this thought felt so joyfully true and loving.

As I felt the joy of this new belief, "I am the beauty that is within me," I sensed the Ascended Masters laughing, overjoyed with "relief," one of them reflecting the thought to me: "Finally, after all the work we have done with, for, and on you!"

Sunday November 4, 2013 – The Lotus and Pearl Vision:

As I meditated this morning, I experienced the crown chakra unfolding. All of a sudden, my consciousness rose out of body, up above and behind my head, as though I were looking down from the ceiling just behind my body.

I "saw" my crown chakra as having very large, beautiful creamy-white petals, and then I saw a beautiful white pearl sitting slightly above the center of the lotus, directly atop my head.

I heard Jesus say to me, "Behold, the pearl of great price."[65]

I thought of the term some people use: "still-point" and thought that this experience was like that, but so much more than that. This experience was energetic and conscious openness, which I now reflect seems very vulnerable, but there was a tremendous strength in this pearl-in-the-lotus experience, as well as perfect peace. Perhaps the perfect peace *is* the strength.

I realized that this vision was significant, especially with Jesus announcing that this was "the pearl of great price," which, in Biblical

---

[65] Please see previous reference, note 32, for this Biblical quote.

terms, refers to the kingdom of God.[66] I believe that Jesus was expressing, among other ideas, the idea of Enlightened Consciousness when he spoke of the kingdom of God.

Eager to know what a pearl in a lotus symbolized in the history of Eastern spirituality, I picked up my cell phone (which usually stays with me, even when I meditate – I know that that does not sound very non-attached!) and searched the internet for "pearl and lotus." Of course, what came up was jewelry! I let go of the search at that time, but later was given significant confirmation of the significance of this vision.

While in that state of oneness with the pearl and the lotus, I realized that the peace I felt was the peace of non-attachment, and that the pearl somehow represents a consciousness that is above the world of form – a consciousness above being attached to this world of materiality.

Needless to say, spending all day in the peace of the pearl of great price, the pearl-in-the-lotus seems like the best place to be, but real life and a need to pay the bills and to keep commitments beckoned me out and beyond the stillness and peace of that moment.

I pray that we may all one day stay in that perfect peace of the priceless pearl-in-the-lotus. I am grateful. I am blessed. Jesus was right that this pearl of great price – the peace of higher consciousness – is worth experiencing and keeping above all else.

---

[66] While engaged in Biblical and theological studies at Vanderbilt University Divinity School, I proposed that Jesus' view of the kingdom of God announced a spiritual reality, an enlightenment paradigm, if you will. I received the Newcombe Prize for my senior project upon graduation with a Master of Divinity degree from Vanderbilt. The title of that project was: "The Word of God, the Body of Christ, and the Kingdom of God: The Church as Divine Presence in the World."

Nov. 7 & 8

The "Ka"

I believe it was Thursday November 7th when I was sitting to meditate, and started praying first. Somehow, I found myself praying for divine power. That startled me, because I haven't believed in asking for divine power, because I believe that asking for divine power instead of focusing on doing divine will can lead us to the "dark side," as it were.

I believe we are meant to focus on asking to be guided to do divine will, and that we will then receive all the strength and power that we need from God in order to accomplish divine will.

Right after praying for divine power, however, I sensed and saw two big, blade-like metal shields behind my back, all the way from the floor to above my shoulders, connected in the center at the base, and pointing outwards like a big "V."

I asked, "What is that?" and I was told it was my Ka.

At that point, I had only once read of a Ka, and so I knew that it had something to do with spiritual energy or spiritual power, but I was really concerned that I had "gone over to the dark side" by asking for power, and the strong, metallic feel of the blades of the Ka really concerned me as well.

So, of course I did an internet search later. I discovered that the concept of the Ka is part of the multi-faceted ancient Egyptian concept of the soul. It is depicted as two arms raised up like goal posts and connected by a bar in-between. The similarity exists then with my vision, which included two arms or branches to the Ka.

Although a variety of understandings are given, from life force to life-giving energy, to "protecting divine spirit of a person,"[67] the *ka* essentially refers to the spiritual energy or power of the individual, so in effect that confirms that, as I had prayed for spiritual power, I had

---

[67] www.britannica.com 2015.

been shown that I had received it, or already possessed it, perhaps.

That day, I also was lifted up above the earth, out of my body, as has happened before. I was shown the view from where the angels look down upon the earth, and I was told:

"We need you to incarnate on earth because we cannot go there."

My sense was this was higher beings – angels – who asked me to incarnate love, but I cannot remember if they used the word 'incarnate.' I know that at some point, I heard a higher being making a pun on incarnate love, the noun, and the command,

"Carol, incarnate love."

What I heard was:

"inCarollove." (Angels have a sense of humor!)

If you think about it, we could all put our names like that, in effect saying "In me let there be love," by saying "In – (name) – Love."

How beautiful will the world be when we all incarnate Love? We will all exist In Love!

The next day, Friday the 8th, when I meditated, I again sensed the Ka, only this time it was made of feathers, and stood up like a feathered, winged "V." I felt better about the feathers than I did about the metal!

This day, I also was lifted up above the earth, and shown how people are in so much emotional and spiritual pain, and told that they need to know to look within themselves to find their answers. Clearly, the message was that I need to help people learn this, which is a central message of this book.

Most people seek answers and solutions outside themselves, but the Tao is the path of inner awareness. This was also an essential aspect of "The Way" of early Christianity, as it was called in the New Testament, although one has to read between-the-lines of the biblical texts to perceive this message.

The Way, the Tao, the path of peace. Only by seeking inside ourselves for that for which we long will we find peace.

The outer manifestations are secondary; not irrelevant, just secondary. When we practice detachment, as both Buddha and Jesus teach us to do, then we can let go of having to have events, objects, and relationships exist or happen a certain way. We are free to decide how we would like to respond to events outside ourselves, but we are much freer when we let go of our attachment to the outcome.

Saturday, November 23, 2013

Vision of the Kingly Mentor

On Saturday, before I meditated, I experienced the kingly aspect of High Priest Melchizedek while I was honoring the Ascended Masters in prayer. So I asked "What does it mean that I am in what is basically a kingly court?" The answer that I received from Melchizedek was that I needed to rule over my life from my Higher Self.

Ahhhh…that meant I had to look at how I was *not* ruling over my life from my higher Self, and one aspect of my life became obvious: in one particular relationship, I was experiencing a lot of pain, because the relationship was out of alignment. Whether one says the relationship was out of alignment because of me or because of the other person does not matter, it became my responsibility to get the relationship back into alignment.

Because of the blessing of being taught by an Ascended Master that I needed to rule my life, I chose to do that. Without that mentoring, I would not have had the strength. However, I thought it through, and decided how I needed to practice non-attachment in the relationship.

That choice set me free from attachment, and I experienced greater love and joy through choosing to be more fully centered.

The fact that the relationship was helping to heal my inner wounded child helped significantly in my spiritual progress. Apparently, healing our inner wounded child (and virtually all of us have one) constitutes an essential step on the spiritual path so that we can fully practice non-attachment to the outer world of form. Without that inner healing, we tend to desire attachment to the people and things which "make" us feel more whole.

After meditating and choosing non-attachment, I had a wonderful, joyful and loving day. Working professionally as an energy healer and spiritual mentor becomes so incredible when we are truly coming from Higher Consciousness, but also just opening up to 'what is' in my personal life with non-attachment felt joyful as well. What a treat!

This joyful state opened me up to be a spiritual mentor for a cashier at Whole Foods. It also opened me up joyfully to receive stinging snowflakes driven by a ferociously cold wind – it reminded me of living in Michigan and learning to love the adventure of dealing with winter weather (well, except maybe the driving!)

How lovely it is to live with non-attachment, for the only replacements for attachment are peace, unconditional love, and joy!

Sunday November 24, 2013

Blissful Vision

On Sunday November 25th, after my early morning prayers, I decided to prepare hot water with the juice of half a lemon and chopped-up bits of fresh ginger and to meditate before taking my morning walk. This was a change for me; prior to this, caffeinated tea with some kind of milky substance (dairy, soy, or almond) had for a couple of decades been my morning cup of attachment.

I renewed my commitment within myself to make that difficult choice of non-attachment in a significant relationship, and then I meditated.

As I honored the Ascended Masters in prayer before meditating, I did what I have learned to do: I believed that we are actually seeing one another, and actually connecting verbally and spiritually.

As I honored Paramahansa Yogananda-ji, I saw a butterfly breaking out of its chrysalis, and flying free. Paramahansa-ji told me: "You have been liberated from imprisonment in the world of form. You have been set free." I knew he was referring to my very difficult and previously painful choice of non-attachment. I felt radiant bliss and love.

Next, I honored Buddha, and what came into my mind was a practice that I have developed as an energy healer of causing the flow of energy in my heart chakra to reverse direction in order to flow, resonate with, and heal my clients as needed. Can you imagine matching the flow of your heart chakra energy with Buddha?

It seemed to me that Buddha was doing this *with* me, or having me do this with him, that is, matching heart chakra flow. Then, the image of the yin-yang symbol came to my mind, and I realized that Buddha was showing me that hearts which resonate with one another in loving partnership will flow together like yin-yang, while each one also stays centered in the divine (represented by the dot on each side).

And then the yin-yang symbol was mirrored, as feelings, thoughts, and intentions are mirrored in relationship, so that the two hearts mirrored one another in sacred balance as the feminine and masculine were balanced within each one, and the love flowed harmoniously because both partners stayed fully centered. What I felt was this incredible loving harmony, and I was experiencing it with Buddha!

In other words, our Higher Selves are capable of attaining this

167

loving harmony all the time, independent of anyone else. We are also capable of experiencing this loving harmony with others who live at this level of non-attachment and purity of intention.

I could feel the love and sheer bliss of being so completely centered that one chooses complete non-attachment to Life in its outer form. I felt utter, complete, *Bliss.*

For the first time in my life, I went into *sheer bliss!* The kind of bliss you hear about, read about, and wonder about – Bliss!

I laughed. I meditated. I stretched out on the carpet and laughed and rolled around and laughed with ecstasy so profound that nothing else mattered.

That day, I maintained a higher level of non-attachment and love and joy than I have ever felt, and more connected than I had felt in a couple of months. Nonetheless, I found myself experiencing slight fears, slight attachments to negative thoughts, and some attachment to particular outcomes. The good news is that I noticed when I was doing so, and that is key! So I am grateful for a renewed sense of Enlightenment Living, which is that ability to balance the pearl in the lotus through non-attachment to the outer world of form.

When I went later to a choir rehearsal for an interfaith Thanksgiving service, the couple leading the rehearsal commented on feeling the energy around me – apparently, bliss can be shared!

Nov. 26, 2013, Tuesday morning Meditation

In my time of prayer and meditation, I experienced Lady Kwan Yin telling me: "Be at peace before you speak." My biggest impression of Lady Kwan Yin when I greet and honor her is that she is very quiet, yet filled with deep, inner wisdom, and surrounded by the energy of peace. I am so grateful for her gentle, wise way of being.

My attention was then turned to these affirmations:

168

I live and move and have my being inside the One Who Is Love;
therefore, all is well.

Others live and move and have their being inside Love, and so I will honor them for their part in the unfolding of Love within and around all of us.

All is Love, therefore all is well.

Love creates this world of Maya, illusion, to give us free will so that we can learn our lessons well. We are co-creators of the illusions around us. Those aspects that neither look nor feel loving are aspects that we get to experience so that we can learn more fully how to choose love.

If we choose love only for ourselves, it will remain illusory.
If we choose love only for others, it will remain elusive.

When we choose to state our preferences for how the flow of love moves through us and through our lives, and yet we also choose to remain non-attached to how the flow occurs, we will simply become part of the flow, directed by the highest good.

When we come from a place of non-attachment, we are like God, who is the Uncreated Self who has no need to feel attachment to any outcome in this world. When we state our preferences (or request our preferences through prayer), we use our gift of free will to energize the flow around us. If we seek to control that flow by *demanding* that which we seek, the energy dries up and no longer supports us in that desire because God is the One Who gives free will. Freedom necessitates giving up making demands and seeking to control.

So, when we lovingly state our preferences and choose to remain non-attached so that the highest good can occur, we allow the Universe to unfold as it is meant, fulfilling universal purposes, not just our own little self-interests.

May the flow of energy guide and direct us into a more love- and light-filled path!

ॐ

November 27, 2013, Wednesday Morning Meditation

Before I meditated, I was attempting to focus on my opening prayers, and sipping my tea (okay, it took me awhile to give it up entirely). My mind kept getting distracted. So, one of the "Higher-Ups" (as I fondly like to refer to the Ascended Masters and Angelic Beings who give me guidance) said to me:

"Stop focusing your mind on the graveyard of the past as well as the graveyard of the future. Instead, plant your mind in the garden of the Now."

Wow! What powerful advice. I had not thought of focusing on the future as focusing on a graveyard, but that is exactly what we do when we start worrying about the future; it becomes a graveyard where all our fears become buried underground to poison the soil for whatever then might or might not grow in future seasons of our lives.

The past being a graveyard seems more obvious to me, and I think, to all of us, simply because the past is over-and-gone, done with – can't change a thing about it. But to think of the future as a graveyard was new to me. I guess my thoughts and ideas about the future were probably all dead-ends!

Of course the message is that life blooms and grows in the fertile soil of the present moment, so why not focus on what is needed now. When our thoughts and our intentions our focused on the Now, our energies are also focused on the Now, and so our present moment becomes more fully energized to give birth to new, good, loving things, events and relationships.

I am grateful that this message came to me during this week in which we celebrate the harvest – Thanksgiving – so what I hear in essence is:

Let's cultivate the garden of the Now
by planting ourselves firmly in it,
and the harvest will yield incredible results!

CHAPTER FIFTEEN: HUMANITY, DIVINITY, AND WHOLENESS

November 29, 2013: Divine Romance

As human beings, we seek to be loved. Whether we are heterosexual, gay, lesbian, bi-sexual, transgender, male or female, we tend to seek love from other human beings. The love we are truly seeking, though, is what many spiritual teachers have termed "The Divine Romance."[68]

This term "The Divine Romance" may be understood numerous ways; I believe I am being helped to understand it through a focus on gender balance and harmony, so all of us can benefit.

No matter what our orientation romantically, physically, and sexually, we are all seeking to be filled with divine love that contains the energies of both the sacred masculine and the sacred feminine. Now, I'm not speaking of relationships in which one person is objectified and worse yet subjugated by another, but I am speaking of sacred partnership, which is egalitarian as well as empowering of both feminine and masculine energies.

The primary starting point for any and all healthy relationships is the Self, that is, our Higher Self, true inner core self, or soul self. This soul self is balanced, harmonious, and complete, like the yin-yang symbol.

To help us understand this point, I'd like to share an affirmation that came to me when I found myself in Paris by the River Seine, with a credit card that was not working to get me French francs (this was in 2000, before Euros were in full circulation). I had a small amount of U.S. dollars on me, and a credit card that was not working

---

[68] (cf. Paramahansa Yogananda, for example, but there are also other books by this title.)

for some reason, a friend who seemed unable to help, and two teenage children in tow. We had traveled to Paris from London, for just a couple of days' visit. The credit card had worked in London!

I sat there by the Seine to get centered, blessed as I was to be near Notre Dame Cathedral, and sitting over the wonderful energy of the river. As I sat there and prayed, I reflected on how I could at least speak some French, and then the affirmation came to me: "All I need I have within me." (It must have been the angels speaking to me – this is just the kind of message my guardian angels would bring!)

I cannot tell you how powerful that affirmation has become for me. It certainly accomplished us getting through that situation just fine, although I don't remember the details. Everything worked out beautifully.

When it comes to relationships, the affirmation "All I need I have within me" provides a healthy starting point as well, because when we seek what we want from outside ourselves, especially from someone else, we are putting a lot of pressure on them to deliver what we feel we want or need.

But, all we need, we have within us. That affirmation takes the pressure off the relationship and puts it onto our sacred selves.

It is important to consider that our own, inner sacred selves are neither just masculine nor just feminine. We need the balance of both energies within ourselves to be whole. When we seek to be loved, to feel loved, and to feel accepted and affirmed, what we are really seeking is Divine acceptance, Divine affirmation, and Divine love, and that Love is both feminine and masculine.

We may think we are looking for a woman or a man, but what we really seek is the energy of love that we feel lacking in ourselves, whether the masculine love energy or the feminine love energy. One is more outwardly active, pushing, strengthening, and the other is more embracing, receiving, and nurturing. We need both energies for loving our own selves completely.

Here is an icon for meditating on the truth of our own inner completeness:

173

All I Need I Have
Within Me

Affirming the yin-yang balance of feminine and masculine love within us can enable us to feel and be complete, or whole. In order to achieve balance and wholeness within ourselves, it may help us all to be able joyfully to affirm:

The Sacred Masculine loves me.
The Sacred Feminine loves me.
I am complete in Divine Love.
I am the Love I seek.
I am loved, I am lovable, and I am loving.
I love myself. I love others.
I love the Sacred Masculine in all his forms.
I love the Sacred Feminine in all her forms.

When we do achieve a sense of our own inner balance, harmony, and completeness, then the loving relationships and partnerships we draw into our lives become healthier and easier to balance as well.

May we be blessed with the fullness of Divine Love that is already within us! May we be made whole through the path of Divine Romance.

December 2013

The "I AM" in the All

The intuition that came to me recently is: The "I AM" is also "The All".

There is no way to separate ourselves completely from the All, for the All is everything which is in God, and the All is God in everything. God is the "I AM" in the All.[69]

This speaks of the Truth that We Are One:

I Am one with others in their pain and suffering.
The All is one with me when I suffer.
I Am one with others in their joy and happiness.
The All is one with me in my joy and happiness.

May you feel the comfort of the "I AM" Presence when you need it most.

May we also learn to share the comfort of the "I AM" Presence with others, because we are One with others in their pain and sorrow as well.

We Are All One in Love – Always.

Born From Above

On Christmas day, 2013, it occurred to me that the concept of "born from above" could be understood in what is for me a totally new

---

[69] Both terms refer to the Presence of the Divine in creation.

way. There is a Biblical text in which Jesus states (John, chapter 3) "you must be born from above."

The Greek word translated "above" can also be translated "again" and so it is often translated that way, "born again." Traditionally, Protestant Christians have understood being "born again" to mean "accepting Christ as your Savior and receiving the Holy Spirit." Being born again has therefore been understood as an event, although, ideally, it leads to changed personhood as well as changed behavior.

For several years, I have believed that Jesus meant "born from above," in the sense of living from our true selves, our souls, the divine presence within us, our Higher Selves, or whatever equivalent term you might use here. This concept is, I believe, vital on our spiritual paths. In other words, being born from above means, in its essence, that instead of living from our ego selves, we live from our Higher Selves.

This past Christmas, this understanding became crystal clear to me because of my "new" understanding of the higher chakras: that being born from above refers to having our crown chakras open, and allowing ourselves to be guided by our Higher Selves through our crown chakras. (This opening of the crown chakra, by the way, can lead to the halo effect of having light emanate from one's crown chakra, so Christian artists who painted halos around saints and the "Holy Family" intuitively perceived and portrayed the light of fully energized crown chakras of the Holy Ones.)

The crown chakra connects us directly with the Divine aspect of ourselves, that is, our Higher Selves, which is also our Bindu, or eighth chakra, the Guru Chakra. The eighth chakra connects us directly with God and Higher Beings. Consciousness from higher realms, higher beings, and Divine energy can flow through the eighth chakra into a fully open and fully energized crown chakra.

This, I believe, constitutes the fullest development of the meaning of the phrase "born from above": that we have opened and blossomed the thousand-petaled lotus of the crown chakra, resulting in our living from this higher plane of consciousness, which comes from above, guided by our own Higher Self or Guru Chakra.

Of course, in the Christian tradition, the concept of being "born again" by accepting Christ as one's savior is also referred to as salvation. Interestingly, most Christians (in my experience as a minister) do not know that the original Greek word which has been translated in English as "salvation" actually means "wholeness," at least as Jesus often used the word when he was healing people.[70]

In other words, instead of focusing on the alternative meaning "born again," perhaps we translate that Greek word *soteria* more accurately along the lines of Jesus' intent of wholeness here when we understand that we can become one with God through higher consciousness flowing "from above" through our crown chakras. This flow of higher consciousness indeed makes us whole by giving birth to us as our Divine Selves, which unites us with God, which is our ultimate salvation.

Self-Realization is salvation. Self-Realization constitutes our ultimate healing as well as our ultimate wholeness.

That Christmas, I felt inspired to focus on Divine Presence within myself as well as others. I was reminded that Jesus was also called "Emmanuel," or "God with us." So, giving birth to Divine Presence within ourselves is exactly what the incarnation of Jesus as the Christ represents. By focusing on the birth of Divine Presence within each of us all the time, we can celebrate the true meaning of Christmas all the time.

Yes, Jesus as the Christ paved the way, but he invites all of us to give birth to Divine Presence through our crown chakras – or to be

---

[70] This is a concept I learned at Vanderbilt Divinity School. From the following site, one learns that Jesus uses the Greek term *soteria* (salvation) in relationship with healings to describe a person's wholeness:

http://spiritualityandchristianity.com/theological-topics/soteria-a-view-of-resurrection-and-wholeness born from above just as he was.

If our religion is something other than Christianity, it does not matter, for this higher consciousness exists in everyone's eighth chakra![71]

Since that Christmas, it has also intuitively come to me that our eighth chakra, our own Higher Selves, is what many of us experience as the "Personal aspect of God." God beyond our own guru chakra is the impersonal aspect of the Divine. So, many people resonate more with the impersonal aspect of the Divine and focus on experiencing the no-self aspect of connecting with Divine energies, while many of us do experience a personal or personified aspect of God. This personal aspect of God appears through our eighth chakra.

When we fully realize the God Presence within us through our eighth chakra, we become truly whole, and we become fully One. This is our true salvation, or wholeness.

Lessons in Mastery: Non-Attachment in Difficult Circumstances

I know I have written about this over and over again, yet many of us resist this lesson: choosing non-attachment to external forms is a necessity on the path to Self-Realization.

When we feel fear or anger, anxiety or extreme emotional hurt, this is a signal that we are holding onto something rather than practicing non-attachment. When we recognize that we are feeling upset, then the first thing we need to do is to identify what it is that we

---

[71] Please remember, my goal here is not to promote Christianity, but rather to highlight the unity of the teachings of all religions at this mystical level, while showing how the Ascended Masters now work together to teach us these higher truths, for we are all One. Re-interpreting Christian tradition is an important aspect of arriving at this higher consciousness of Unity.

are seeking to hold onto, such as a certain person treating us a certain way, or getting paid a certain amount for our work, or overcoming cancer, or whatever it may be.

Once we have identified what we're holding onto, then we can ask the Divine for help letting go. Letting go, of course, isn't easy, but asking for divine help makes it easier.

For Christmas 2013, I actually asked my family members to get me artwork and statues of Buddha, who has, in his Ascended Master form, directly helped me with spiritual issues before, especially non-attachment.

The Sunday after Christmas 2013, I was indeed struggling with something deeply emotional and I felt a million miles away from peace. So, I picked up the medicine Buddha sculpture that I had been given a few days before, and asked Buddha to help me with non-attachment. I asked, "How do I deal with this?"

The reply I got was first:

"Let go of desire."

Of course, I've heard that before, but this was a case in which desire was extremely hard for me to let go. So, I asked for help letting go of desire, and *Buddha answered that I just needed to let God know that I love him/her more than the desire that I was holding onto.*

So, I began the practice of letting God know what I desire, but also then telling God that I desire God more than the desire I was holding onto. This works! It works with money, with relationships, and with health. For instance, one can affirm: I love God, and I appreciate money. My preference is to be one with God, and to be fully supported in my financial needs. Letting go of everything else is easier when we trust that God and the Universe will honor our preferences in ways that enable us to fulfill our divine potential on earth.

I am so grateful to Buddha for teaching this lesson this way,

179

because we get to express our desires to God without shame or guilt or blame, and we get to remember to put God first.

Obviously, non-attachment in difficult situations can seem very challenging, so I hope this technique will help you.

One of the wonderful gifts of this approach is that, if we tell God several times a day that we love God and that we desire God more than anything else, it not only changes us for the better, it changes our lives for the better.

May you be richly blessed with non-attachment through the pure energy of devotion, and may your devotion purify and transform you!

Purity and the Essence of Form

Recently, The Ascended Masters have reminded me directly, but gently, of the need for purity on the path of Self-Realization.

Virtues like purity are angelic. When I learned to work with the Archangels of the Seven Rays after my Enlightenment Vision in 2010 (initiation), it was largely thanks to a chart that my Reiki teacher had sent me,[72] which showed the virtues associated with each Archangel.

Archangel Gabriel is the Archangel of purity, and that virtue has always felt essential to me in so far as having the ability to work with archangels and to channel the Seven Rays to others for their healing.

Well, recently, I was reminded that Archangel Gabriel is the Archangel of not only purity but also hope, and that the Crystal-White Ray associated with Gabriel is the Ray of Ascension. In other words, in order to Ascend to higher realms, to higher levels of consciousness,

---

[72] From *The Law of Life*, Book II.

and to Self-Realization, we need to be pure (as well as hopeful!).

What does pure mean? This morning, I asked that very question during my time of prayer and meditation, and the answer that I received was this:

Purity is the sacrifice of form
in order to achieve pure essence.

Here the word 'form,' refers to the material world and all of its associated ideas, desires, fantasies, and projected realities. The world of form embodies Spirit in an infinite variety of forms, yet the forms themselves are empty, just as Maya is merely an empty Illusion. The world of form, or the material world, which is also called Maya, is temporary. The essence expressed in each form is eternal. This essence is Spirit.

Essence is a word which refers to spiritual qualities, just like the virtues of honesty, integrity, purity, and compassion. More than that, essence is the expression of Divine Self in the Being-ness of the Universe. So, the essence of the Divine is in each one of us.

Expressing pure essence is expressing God.

The Divine qualities of self-giving, self-sacrifice, putting others first are in particular very pure. What a joy it can be to express these qualities.

Today I had the joy of being prompted (by inner, higher guidance) to ask a "homeless" man who was sitting out in the freezing cold selling *Street Sense* (the homeless paper in DC) what it would take for him to go home to get out of the cold. (His name is Earl, and in previous conversations, I had found out that he was no longer homeless, but selling these papers is his source of income.)

Earl made it clear that he needed to earn some more money, maybe $10. I said, "If I give you $10 will you go home?" Earl replied, "Yes, I've been sitting outside here in the cold since 9 am." (It was about 5 pm at the time.) I gave Earl $10 and said, "Go home. God

181

bless you."

Now, this was not me being kind; this was the essence of Divine Kindness expressing itself through me. I am just the empty vessel through which compassion expressed itself. What great joy it was to experience the Divine Compassion expressing itself through me and to see Earl being blessed.

This is not something for which I can take credit. This was not my compassion, not me being "me," but God being who God is because I allowed God to act through me. Now, that IS a joy!

May you find the purity of God within you, so that you can ascend to higher states, and reach that final state of pure love, peace, and bliss called Self-Realization!

January 2014

A Vow, a Spiritual Name, and the Formation of a Spiritual Community

Early in January of 2014, I was challenged by someone else on the spiritual path to take the vows of a Swami: the vows of poverty and celibacy. This person presented this message as though it were coming from the same Ascended Masters who teach me, and presented himself as being Self-Realized, and therefore I "should" do what he was telling me. He also told me to stop eating eggs, to wear Swami robes, and to take a spiritual name.

Now, I have lived in relative poverty several times in my life at this point, and I have spent many years being celibate. I think God knows that I am willing to do both as needed for the spiritual path. I also have no desire to block the flow of love toward myself in whatever way God would like to send it to me.

I experienced profound pain as this person insisted that he was receiving this message from the Ascended Masters, and at first, I felt guilted into agreement, since he also said that I would not become Self-Realized unless I do so. Please understand, this person has no leadership role in any spiritual community, and this person is not a Swami himself. But I respect this person as a truly beautiful spiritual human being, whose experiences in life happen to be very limited by physical conditions.

I agonized over this request – well, more of an instruction on the path. I spoke with my most spiritually advanced friends – at the time, I had three who were at about the same stage of connection or purity or intuition as myself. (Now I have four or more!) I also discussed it with a friend who pointed out that I don't believe in celibacy as a large scale practice, because it contributes to the denigration of women, to rape (a gang rape in India was prominent in the news around that time), and to the molestation of children as has occurred in the Catholic Church. Suppressing one's sexuality does not seem either healthy or spiritual to me. Transmuting it may be ideal, but most human beings are not ready for this!

My friends were generally supportive of either my taking Swami vows, or my starting a new community "myself" that would be different than traditional religious communities. Thank God for enlightened friends!

I finally realized that, if I am to become Self-Realized, I cannot get my answers from the Ascended Masters through someone else, because that would not be my True Self connecting with God through the Higher Beings; it would be the other person connecting. I also did not think that I was doing something for God if it made me feel sad. It made sense to me that what I joyfully perceive as what I am meant to do directly from God is alone what will lead me to Self-Realization, rather than having to go through someone else.

After a good night's sleep, I awoke with a sense of joy, as well as a sense of what vow I would be willing to take. I joyfully announced it to my friends:

I vow to live a life of non-attachment to the world of form, seeking union with the Divine Mother/Father through unconditional love, and embodying unconditional love in service to others.

This felt right! This vow felt joyful! Non-attachment leaves us free to receive as well as to let go. Union with God focused on unconditional love felt like the joyful, celebratory approach to life, faith, and all things spiritual! Service to others is the legacy I received from my parents and I find great joy in the thought of emphasizing embodying unconditional love as the focal point in service to others.

My friends were happy for me, and supported me in the idea of starting a new spiritual community. I met with two friends to start shaping a vision statement, mission statement, and core values. We came up with the name Self-Realization Community. Not to be confused with the Self-Realization Fellowship founded by Paramahansa Yogananda,[73] the Self-Realization Community[74] emphasizes community both as part of its spiritual practice as well as the gender inclusive nature of the term.

Even though it is wonderful, I could not see myself in the Self-Realization Fellowship, because even if you get high up in it, I learned that you are only allowed to teach the teachings of Paramahansa Yogananda as he passed them on before he died. What to do, when you are being taught directly by Ascended Masters of many faiths, including Paramahansa-ji?

The only reasonable solution seemed to be to create a new spiritual community which blended together different religious traditions in order to announce to the world: We Are One.

---

[73] https://www.yogananda-srf.org/ The Self-Realization Fellowship reflects the beautiful teachings of Paramahansa Yogananda in a most faithful way. I am grateful to them for the many publications of Paramahansaji's writings.

[74] http://selfrealizationcommunity.org/

That is the message of the Ascended Masters who work with me: We Are One. This is also what we affirm to one another during services of Celebration of the Self-Realization Community: We Are One.

We human beings no longer have any need for religious barriers, or dogmatic adherence to sacred texts; we have living masters who guide us from above, including guiding us to the sacred texts of different religious traditions as needed for our learning and spiritual growth.

As if to confirm this inner guidance to start a new spiritual community, I was meditating one morning not long after this decision was made, and I felt moved to bow down before God and the Ascended Masters. I felt a mantle placed upon my shoulders (just a feeling, not a physical 'reality'), and heard them say "Receive your crown." (Not a glorifying crown, but a purifying one: a crown of light which cleanses and purifies as is so necessary on the spiritual path!)

I asked for a spiritual name and heard,

"*Lamada.*"

I asked, "Lamada?"

And then I heard,

"Lambda."

I asked, "Lambda?"

(As I joked later to my daughter, apparently I am a little hard of hearing on the spiritual plane as well as the earthly plane!)

I then knew intuitively that I was supposed to take the "b" from Lambda and add it into "Lamada."

Accustomed to searching on the internet for verifications of these spiritual experiences, I picked up my phone and googled "lamada." Nothing came up, except the possible alternate spelling of "Lambada." I had never heard the word "Lambada" before, so I searched for its meaning.

Oh, joy and laughter – I landed on a site which explained that the Lambada is an erotic Brazilian couple's dance!

185

At first, all I could think of was how so many Christians would be shocked at that being my "spiritual" name.

And then I thought of the Supreme Divine couple: Shiva and Shakti. I thought, "Perfect! My name refers to the dance of Shiva and Shakti in creation – the flow of Love in Life – the flow of Divine Love through the Universe! I love it!"

I also love to dance, and performed liturgical dance in churches both as a teenager and as an adult. The name "Lambada"[75] therefore resonates deeply with me.

Ever since I was a teenager, I have also wanted to be called "Nonnie" as a grandmother, so I searched online for the meaning of "Nonnie" as well. One site listed "Nonnie" both as meaning "grandmother" and as being a derivative of Eleanor, meaning "ray of sun, shining light."

Perfect! Nonnie Lambada – a ray of light dancing through the universe with Shiva and Shakti. Now all I "needed" was a third name – something with "ananda" which means "bliss."

I thought about "premananda," which means "love-bliss," but I didn't yet see myself as existing in a perpetual state of loving bliss, and it didn't feel quite right, either.

During the summer of 2014, someone highly intuitive said they were getting "Satananda" for me, which means "truth-bliss," and that felt better. However, I don't feel fond of that spelling, as the letters for "Satan" appear in there. Fortunately, "satya" also means "truth," so "Satyananda" would work well. I love discovering the truths of the Universe!

So, someday, I hope to go by the name "Nonnie Lambada Satyananda," but I do believe I will have to earn it!

---

[75] My pronunciation of the name "Lambada," based on what I heard from the ascended realms, emphasizes a different syllable than the name of the dance. For "my" name, the first syllable is emphasized rather than the second syllable.

Later, during the summer of 2014, I felt challenged by the same individual who had wanted me to take Swami vows. This led to more feelings of upset and deep soul-searching.

What became clear to me out of this deep soul-searching is that the closer we grow to God, the more we see God in others. If we cannot see God in others, it is not something we can merely blame on them, for it is our responsibility to see everyone's soul Self, not just their ego-self. The more we let go of our ego-self, the easier it is to see other people's soul-Selves. So, the closer we grow to Union with God, the easier it becomes to see God in others.

In 2010, when I had had my Enlightenment Vision, it changed me so much, that I had wondered what that made me; I couldn't believe I was a full guru, because I could see my own ego clearly lurking about. So, that summer I asked "What does this make me?" The answer I had received was: "guru-doula."

How delightful – someone who brings the light to help us give birth to the Divine Self inside ourselves.

In the summer of 2014, when I was experiencing this deep self-doubt after being challenged by the spiritual person who apparently did not see God in me, I again asked, "Who am I? What is my role?"

The answer I again received was: "guru-doula."

What has become clear to me is that my role with clients, my role in life, and my role in the Self-Realization Community is to help people see the Divine within themselves and to give birth to the Divine within and through themselves. This is what I love to do!

I finally felt at peace.

February 3, 2014

The Divine Self

We humans often become so confused about our sense of self and our relationship with God. When we look at ourselves through the eyes of ego, we take credit for who we are and what we do.

When we begin to see ourselves through the eyes of our Souls, or Higher Selves, it is as though a veil has been removed, and we begin to see that anything "good" which we find in ourselves is, in truth, not "us" (or "me") at all!

Rather, through a higher, soulful perspective - a God's eye view - we see that the beauty, the kindness, the compassion, the wisdom, the intelligence, and the purity that is within us, all constitutes "Who God Is In Us."

If you think about it, kindness is kindness in me, in you, and in everyone else. Gentleness is gentleness in you, in me, and in others. It's all the same. So, God as kindness, God as gentleness, and God as Unconditional Love is essentially the same in all of us, even if expressed somewhat differently.

When we use the "I AM" statements as a tool for becoming aware of our Divine Oneness, we can therefore affirm: "I AM the beauty (kindness, love) that is within me." By this statement, we affirm that everything beautiful, loving, kind, talented, and good within us truly comes from God, for we did not make ourselves.

Furthermore, our actions, choices, and words, when they are loving, wise, and true, also come from God. Karma yoga teaches the principle of union with God through engaging in selfless acts of service, through which the devotee becomes aware that it is "not I, but God who acts through me." When we empty ourselves of ego, we allow more space for God to be Present within us, and therefore for God to act through us.

In actuality, when we experience something wonderful as an

188

aspect of ourselves, we are experiencing "Who God Is" within us.

It is necessary for us to become "fully human" before we become "fully divine," or allow the flowering of our Divine Self, which is Self-Realization. Becoming fully human includes becoming fully aware of the truths of our own inner being, and expressing this inner Self openly, honestly, purely, and freely.

Becoming fully divine necessitates that we begin fully to see "Who God Is In Us," as well as connecting with "Who God Is Beyond Us," so that we are able to allow the full expression of the true blending, or union of both.

May you become aware of your own inner Divine Self, and may you see the Divine Self in others.

There are stages on this path to Self-Realization, and right now, I am going through a stage of purifying and releasing emotional attachment (or so I was just told by the Higher-Ups!). Such release generally entails dealing with relationships in which we have high emotional attachment to outcomes.

In other words, this stage can feel really tough, emotionally speaking, because we get to learn non-attachment to significant life events, accomplishments, and relationships – not just non-attachment to mere objects, pleasures, and possessions. Non-attachment on all levels becomes necessary for advancement on the spiritual path.

That same day, I did not receive something I wanted from someone else (attachment.) When I complained to God about not getting what I had been wanting from that person, through my crown chakra I was invited to rise up to join the Ascended Masters, who were saying,

"You know what, it does not matter. What you want so badly, does not even matter. Come up here - we're having a party!"

189

Talk about motivating non-attachment!

This reminds me of a truth that I was taught to share with a client in the fall of 2013:

If we could see how events and relationships in our lives will unfold from a God's eye view, we would be happy, so why not go ahead and be happy anyway?![76]

On the higher level of consciousness, there is always a sense of completeness and unity with the Divine, which is redemption. When we can raise the vibration of our thoughts and intentions, we redeem our whole selves by living as our Higher Selves. Redemption and Self-Realization are essentially one and the same thing. No one else can do it for us, but they can pave the way, and lead the way, as Christ and Buddha (and others) have done.

May you find your redemption in the higher realms, where, quite probably, they will throw you a party! Down here, we are asked to bring that very party to others - not necessarily a pleasure party, but a party of incredible love and acceptance and celebration of each and every person on our path. And yes, a little (or a lot) of pleasure just might be involved, even though it's not the point.

Life is a celebration of redemption - union with the Divine in and through all situations, in all times and places. So, let's celebrate, because Shiva and Shakti are present within us, and they are lovingly dancing through life with us!

---

[76] This reminds me of the wise words of the young hotel owner in the movie "The Best Exotic Marigold Hotel," who says: "It will get better before the end, and if it's not better yet, it's not the end!"

CHAPTER SIXTEEN: CONSCIOUSNESS: EXPERIENCED, EXPLAINED & EXPANDED

Lessons From Above: How the Shift in Consciousness of December 21, 2012 Changed My Life

Lesson One: The Shift

As we approached December 21, 2012, I had the mindset that we human beings would be making a shift in consciousness, as though this was something we were capable of achieving on our own, or with God's help, but still something we worked on.

What I discovered, or heard, as I meditated on 12/21/12, was that we were invited to ascend.

"This is an invitation to ascend."

When we ask or choose to ascend, the gateway of consciousness is now open to a higher, "heavenly" realm, where we will encounter Helpers, Beings of Light who will communicate with us. They will answer our spiritual questions as needed to help us fulfill a higher purpose in life.

The Shift is not something we do; rather, the Shift is the Opening of the Gateway of Consciousness, and all who are ready to ascend are welcome to ascend. If you have ascended before, then this is easy. If you have not yet ascended, the invitation is to begin a spiritual practice which will take you there.

Lesson Two: Ascending

The next day, I repeatedly felt the nudge to meditate. Each

time I meditated, and even when not meditating, if I thought about ascension, then my consciousness ascended and I was aware of the Helpers, who may also be called Friends of Light.

"You are welcome here. You are welcome anytime."

The Gateway is open so that we can attain a higher consciousness, with access to help from the Friends of Light at any time. Some people might choose to call them angels or angelic beings or part of the host of heaven. Others might choose to call them Spirit Guides. Whatever your religion, they are waiting for you and they would like to help you.

"All you have to do is to focus your intention on ascension, and your attention on your Brow Chakra. There you will ascend."

Lesson Three: The Experience of Ascension

After ascending this new gateway a few times, I found myself seeing the setting change, from a peaceful place where Light Friends were sitting and meditating, to stepping stones made of puffy white clouds in a blue sky, and I was hopping from cloud to cloud. My being was lighter and more maneuverable than on earth, but what struck me was that the 'reality' of this setting changed as soon as I had a different image in my mind.

So, I asked: "Is it always like that up here?" I was thinking that my image of heaven was kind of solid compared to that, and not quite so instantly changeable.

"Yes, it is. This reality is made of shared consciousness. We often agree on what kind of setting we prefer, and share that, but new ones and visitors often come to play. When we choose a setting, our

consciousness creates it instantaneously up here, and we can do that together."

Lesson Four: The Reason for Ascension

"Why do we get to ascend whenever we would like?"

"So that we can help you; we are here to guide you into a higher consciousness, and so that you may one day permanently ascend. Before that, you have much work to do to transform yourself, as well as to help others.

Each moment that you need help with self-transformation, we will be available."

Lesson Five: The Nature of God and the Universe

"What is this realm?" I asked.

"This realm is a higher level of consciousness. All realms of consciousness have varying degrees of revelation of the Light, the True Consciousness, The Revelation of God."

I asked: "Who is God? Or should I ask 'What is God?'"

"God is the Unrevealed."[77]

---

[77] I now understand that this most likely referred to the concept of God as the "Unborn." That is, God beyond all Universes, and beyond all other levels of reality, where God would only be experienced as "revealed." So, the "Unrevealed" refers to God as the Absolute, the Unborn, the Uncreated, the Unmoved Mover.

"The Unrevealed?" I struggled with that one.

"If God is unrevealed, then how do we get to know God? And why is God so into revelation, at least from a Judeo-Christian perspective?" My struggles began to be articulated.

"The Revelation of God is through the Spirit, the Aum, the Word, the vibratory essence of Creation. That is the presence, or ongoing revelation of God in the universe. The expression of the Word, the Spirit, the Aum, happens in many ways through 'inanimate' beings, events, and energies.

"The Revelation of God in human beings is often referred to as Christ-Consciousness or Buddha-Consciousness. It may also be called Consciousness of the Light, or Light Consciousness, although it has many dimensions, including heart-consciousness, spiritual-consciousness, and Incarnation through activity."

"If God is the Unrevealed, then how do we get to be with God?"

"When we learn to vibrate at a higher frequency, we will all one day be ready to let go of the illusion of separation, and the revelation will no longer be necessary, because we will be in the still, calm center which is God. Go to the still, calm, center, and there you will find God. The Alpha and the Omega refer to the end of this realm of revelation, where darkness interplays with Light, and so the True Light is often hidden, until we learn to receive the Revelation of the Light.

"In the meantime, people often play with shadows, but you can be playing with rainbows. Ascension and revelation are about playing with the light, the Rainbow Light of God."

ॐ

February 3, 2014

Experiences in Expanded Consciousness on the Way to Self-Realization

Last fall, I had the experience of the "pearl in the lotus," which I experienced as the bliss of non-attachment. Just recently, I read that the pearl refers to the Bindu, or eighth chakra, which is beyond the crown chakra.   From what I read online, expanded consciousness follows the connection with Bindu, and precedes Samadhi, which is Self-Realization, and then Moksha, which is full Liberation and God-Consciousness.[78] I am truly grateful for this website sent to me by a friend; yet another confirmation of the vision I had last fall!

This same friend, who was a devotee of Swami Rama for 20 years, taught me that the phrase "*Om mani padme hum*" can be translated: "the jewel in the lotus." Here, jewel and pearl could be considered interchangeable. So, this phrase provides another confirmation of the vision of "my" Bindu as a pearl above the lotus of "my" crown chakra.[79]

Reading the fact that this level of connection with Higher Consciousness can lead to expansion of one's consciousness was very reassuring to me, because of my recent experiences of expanded consciousness and awareness during times of meditation. In other words, I read about such expansions of consciousness *after* experiencing them, so yet again, I received confirmation of these visions.

---

[78] This information can be found here on this site: http://www.swamij.com/yoga-vedanta-tantra.htm

[79] This same friend taught me that, in Tantric thought, the jewel in the lotus refers to an obvious sexual parallel. Perhaps both are true!

I have previously had experiences of briefly becoming the consciousness of a small animal like a mouse. Recently, I had the experience of being (during a meditative vision) on a ship in the middle of the ocean, and then falling in and facing my greatest fear of the ocean: being bitten by a shark.

Immediately, though, rather than going through the agony of the pain and fear and resenting the shark, I became the shark, and knew, of course, that I had bitten a human being. Then I became the ocean, and sensed the teeming life in the ocean - amazing how it is brimming with life forms on all levels - microscopic on up.

During another meditation, I was standing on a cliff, and then jumped off, and instead of falling down, splat, I was floating as if I had jumped out of an airplane. Then I became the air.

Yes, I became the air, at least, the consciousness of the air. I felt amazed at how much is going on in air. Particles rising and falling and blowing and interacting - so many different kinds of particles; apparently air is "busy" all the time. Who knew?! Well, I am sure some scientists know, but maybe not from inside the consciousness of the air!

Then I became the cliff. I did not spend much time in the consciousness of being a cliff. I also spent some time being inside the consciousness of a tree, although I found it hard to get there. It was easier to perceive the consciousness of a bird in a tree, but then I shed my own body-consciousness to become the tree and one with its consciousness. I have to say that I did not feel very comfortable with the stiffness I felt as a tree -very dry and stiff. Again, it was easier to experience the tree's consciousness of other things, like birds on its branches and air blowing by and the sun shining on it. The dry brittle feeling of the tree itself was strange to me.

At some point (I realize this description may be out-of-order from the actual stream of expanded consciousness I experienced during meditation), I went from being air to rising up to the edge of the earth's atmosphere, which felt very different from the air near the ground. There, the "air" is "aware" of being a boundary, which is cold on the outside, while being bombarded with different particles that flow through its "thinness."

Next, I became space - well, "I" was out in space, but my consciousness was the consciousness of space. What amazed me there was that the particles (or solar wind, or whatever the technical name is for particles and waves of light and radiation) that pass through space are felt by space, and that space experiences them as "messages." In other words, space somehow knows the source of these energies and particles, as well as their nature, and what connections they are making throughout the universe. (I know this sounds strange, and to the uninitiated, unbelievable.)

My conclusion is what I have intuitively believed for many years: that consciousness exists throughout the universe. Or, as I intuited many years ago: the universe is organized consciousness.

I have only recently learned that this is a belief in Tantra. Tantric philosophy posits that the universe is composed of energy and consciousness. Hinduism expresses the concept that the universe is comprised of Shiva (the Absolute, unchanging, uncreated) and Shakti (pure energy). Shiva being the male principle, and Shakti being the female principle, Shakti and Shiva were originally united, before splitting apart.

I find this fascinating, because there is a Hebrew Bible scholar, Phyllis Trible, who wrote *Eve and Adam*, and pointed out that in Hebrew, it is clear that the original Adam was one being comprised of the male and female aspects, and then was split into two, implying an original wholeness through the unity of the masculine and feminine. Echoes of Shiva and Shakti therefore resonate in the Hebrew meaning of the name Adam, or "Adham," which means a human being inclusive of both genders.[80]

As an energy healer who experiences the combination of the

---

[80] For Trible's scholarly and precise analysis, please see, for instance: https://theology4me.wordpress.com/2012/03/11/eve-and-adam-genesis-2-3-reread-phyllis-trible-copyright-1973-by-andover-newton-theological-school/

Presence of both energy and consciousness during healings, I have also long thought of "God" as being a loving energy consciousness that permeates creation. That, of course, would also be Shiva (consciousness) and Shakti (energy).

On the spiritual path of wholeness through Self-Realization, then, we seek to unite with Shiva and Shakti, to fulfill both male and female principles within ourselves. The ultimate consciousness is the awareness of the uncreated Bliss of the union of the two as one, the Absolute which exists beyond the world of form.

The highlight of my adventures in expanded consciousness occurred when, from outer space, I perceived a broad ray of pure white light, and I was invited to become one with that ray of light. The only "problem" with this was that, in order to become one with it, I had to completely drop my "body/sense of self as a human being/separate entity." It took me a couple of tries to be able to do that. Once I became one with the ray of light, I became aware of particles streaming through it, of directionality, of the wave aspect of it, and then, I heard:

"Welcome to pure potential."

That, I believe, is the union of Shiva and Shakti. The Absolute. The One. Only, as I experienced it, the One was not in its unmoved form; rather, it was streaming from its Source aspect into the Universe as Shakti and Shiva united. It seemed to me that energy/consciousness of Shiva and Shakti was streaming along the edge of the universe, bringing the creative power of the Creator as it traveled at light speed.

(I have also experienced consciousness outside this universe, seeing it as a blue-ish infinity symbol, a figure-eight that is also twisted

198

like a Mobius strip. I realize that shape may not fit the concept of the Big Bang, but I think there must be an important metaphor in the visual – something about the universe folding back in on itself.)

Later, it became clear to me that the original split of Shiva and Shakti is the apparent split of energy and consciousness; the two dance together throughout creation, not really separate yet with space or separation between them as though they are a dancing yin-yang symbol, whirling and revolving throughout the universe. It is not, I believe, actually possible entirely to separate energy and consciousness, yet they represent the dance of Shiva and Shakti, as the one "sends" out the other, and then re-unites with it in the world of form.

This could also be expressed by the Yin-Yang symbol, which of course has a small dot of the opposite color within the two sides, which do represent the feminine and masculine aspects.

Perhaps the universe is very Tantric after all, with the original sending out of energy/consciousness to create it being metaphorically understood as the original thrusting of the male principle into the female principle who then gives birth to form out of the active re-uniting of consciousness and energy in new ways. Thus, the universe becomes the very pregnant womb of God (or the Goddess)!

While the original Union of Shiva and Shakti might be called "sexless" in the sense of not being split into two genders, the original creative act is the separating and uniting of the two, which results in this whole amazing and wonderful universe on an on-going basis.

Our end goal, spiritually speaking, however, is to unite the two principles within us in peace and wholeness, and become One with the Absolute beyond form, and so, dropping the concept of sex and gender ultimately results in becoming the True Self, the Avatar, the Uncreated, which is always capable of creating whenever and whatever is needed in this world of form.

May you find love and peace and bliss on your journey of expansion into Ultimate Consciousness.

ॐ

The Teacher Voice shared with me:

Consciousness is undivided.

True consciousness has no divisions in it; everything is the "I AM" expressed in one form or another. The Aum which is the vibratory essence of creation sent forth as the Shakti energy, remains intimately connected with the "I AM," the essence of Shiva, the consciousness of all that is.

Sometimes people experience the connections of consciousness across time and space, beyond one body/mind/spirit being and into or with another mind/body/spirit being, whether human or otherwise. Psychics, intuitives, psychic intuitives, shaman, many energy healers, and those who have attained a higher consciousness beyond enlightenment, all experience "knowing" which cannot be explained to the rational mind. Too many of us experience this to dismiss it, except out of ignorance or fear.

Most of the time, we human beings experience dis-connection, separation, limitation and "personal point of view" as our own conscious experiences. That is largely due to choosing to limit our awareness to the talk which happens in our left brains. Our left brain awareness is mostly rational, self-oriented, analytical, and verbal.[81]

Our right brains are more visionary and connected, but we teach children in our culture to be left-brain dominant in most schools. Think for a moment, if you will, how little time is spent in music, art, and drama at schools, especially now in the days of budget cut-backs. Most of us have our creativity stifled to some degree, and have therefore not learned to trust it.

While Einstein said "Imagination is more important than

---

[81] For an excellent expression of right-brain and left brain consciousness, please see Dr. Jill Bolte-Taylor's video on TEDTalk or her book by the same title: *My Stroke of Insight.*

knowledge," we are also taught to dis-trust imagination, for it is not a left-brain activity, and is therefore, not rational.

However, consciousness consists of more than just rationality: even in our own minds consciousness consists of perceptual signals such as light, pain, color, pleasure, as well as feelings such as grief, joy, happiness, and emotions such as love and fear.

Philosophers employ the term "arational" to refer to consciousness that is neither purely rational, nor irrational. Beyond the limiting conception of rationality as falling on a linear spectrum between two poles: rational and irrational, philosophers have recognized a third dimension: consciousness which is arational. For instance, a particular feeling or desire may not be considered either rational or irrational. An individual belief may consist of an arational thought, such as "God loves me."

Clearly, the dichotomy of "rational" and "irrational" is too limiting for our experiences of consciousness. The dichotomy also implies the duality of "good" and "bad."

For instance, many of us experience intuitive flashes of inspiration, such as that "great idea" that pops into our heads, or music that seems to create itself within us, or visions of what could appear on a canvas, or visions of what could be created through owning a business or through teaching a class. We experience creative consciousness within us. We experience visionary consciousness within us. Many of us even have mystical visions as well.

Consciousness comes in many forms, yet it is never limited by any one form in which it is expressed. All consciousness remains unlimited because it is connected to its Source: the Divine Consciousness which is eternal and beyond the limits of this universe of form.

All consciousness remains part of the Aum which is the vibration of Shakti dancing with Shiva through the universe, or the Divine Mother/Father "speaking" reality into being. Or perhaps Shiva and Shakti are not only dancing but also singing the universe into being, or at least chanting life into being. Shiva speaks, Shakti sings, and together they dance worlds into being!

When our consciousness becomes increasingly open to and then attuned to Divine Consciousness, we are able increasingly to perceive the unity of all being, and of all consciousness, without limit, and without divisions. The separation is an illusion; a temporary construct, if you will, in order to enable us to attain mastery of our own consciousness. Ultimately, when that mastery is attained we become aware of larger consciousness and we discover the truth: We are all One.

When I previously experienced the consciousness of different aspects of the universe, my left brain thought of my experiences as "crazy." My right brain just accepted these experiences as real.

I confess to feeling some comfort, delight, and gratitude as I recently read this description of Christ-Consciousness in the glossary in Paramahansa Yogananda's *Where There Is Light*:

"Christ Consciousness is the projected consciousness of God immanent in all creation ... Kutastha Chaitanya, the cosmic intelligence of Spirit everywhere present in creation. It is the universal consciousness, oneness with God, manifested by Jesus, Krishna, and other avatars. Great saints and yogis know it as the state of Samadhi meditation wherein their consciousness has become identified with the intelligence in every particle in creation; they feel the entire universe as their own body."[82]

I so appreciate receiving after-the-fact confirmations of these visions! This so resonates with what I experienced, though my vision was to a lesser degree. Perhaps I was approaching an experience of Samadhi, but did not know it.

---

[82] Paramahansa Yogananda, *Where There Is Light*, (Los Angeles: Self-Realization Fellowship), 2000, p. 195.

One morning after receiving these insights, I again experienced bliss during my meditation, or perhaps, directly at the end of my meditation. I was affirming that I would balance that pearl of great price above my crown chakra, except the words that formed in my consciousness were: "I will balance that egg."

Immediately, I heard,

"You'd better balance that egg or you will have egg on your face!"

What bliss to have a joke about the difference between ego-consciousness and enlightened consciousness come through my crown chakra! I felt blissful humor - which is beyond any humor I have felt before. The Ascended Masters have a great sense of humor!

The Higher Ups are sharing an affirmation today to help us attain this expansive, ecstatic consciousness:

I empty myself, and I AM.

April 24, 2014

What Is Real?

I love how this question was famously asked and answered in the children's book, *The Velveteen Rabbit.* The question arose as I was working with a young client a few weeks ago. As she was experiencing her boyfriend's family, and wondering about the nature of her relationship with them, the question of what is real arose.

So often, in our ego-based human cultures, we deal with pretense. People often put on facades and project out to the world who we would like the world to believe we are. Relationships often become defined in certain ways that give us either a sense of control or a sense of comfort.

What does the world of Spirit have to share with us on the subject of what is real?

Well, as I asked for the blessing that this young woman needed to receive at the end of energy healing (a practice of blessing that I do with clients), what came to me (along with the rest of the blessing which was for her) was the intuition:

The root of reality is truth, consciousness, and love.

This brings us back to the concepts of Shiva and Shakti: Energized Consciousness, and Conscious energy, and adds two elements – Truth and Love. The energy of our Source is loving energy, and the consciousness of our Source is Truth.

Knowing the truth is so helpful. I have met many people who hide from the truth one way or another, or who hide the truth from others. To some extent, I believe we all do this – or have done this in the past.

But being brave enough to face the truth of our own being, the truth of someone else's being, and the truths of our lives is essential on our spiritual paths.

How can we know what is real if we don't find the courage to face the truth? Facing the truth brings us closer to what is really real – the world of Spirit, and that world is so loving, we can hardly imagine it.

The reality of this love is that it is something which never binds us, but from which we can never escape. We always exist inside this field of loving consciousness, but sometimes our vibration is so low that we cannot feel it, and we feel separate from it.

What is real? Truth, love, and consciousness. The more we choose to open our consciousness to both Truth and Love, the more our consciousness resonates with the Divine consciousness of Shiva and Shakti – the very essence and power of the Universe.

May you be filled with this Truth and Love, so that you may live within it forever.

ॐ

April 24, 2014

The Fundamental Nature of Reality and the Key to Enlightenment

This week is transformational for me. Buddha has graciously worked with me through what has been the most difficult issue of my life. What that issue is for me doesn't really matter; please substitute whatever your most difficult issue may be - whether it is self-esteem, life-threatening disease, loss of a loved one, fear of being alone, desperation in romance, career failure, addiction, financial problems, failure in important relationships, or whatever the biggest challenge of your life might be.

My desire for a certain potentially important outcome in my life was thwarted, for the umpteenth time, so it seems. I felt deeply hurt. I couldn't sleep. Yet, in the early morning hours, I clearly heard the affirmation, "All is well."

I have heard that affirmation many times before, from other people, from the Ascended Masters and my guardian angels and whoever has helped me at different times. This time, of course, I found it difficult to feel and to believe, although I knew it to be true.

After a few hours and attempts at meditation and prayer, feeling led by Buddha, I picked up a book called *Buddha,* by Karen Armstrong, which my daughter had given me for Christmas. Flipping through, I felt drawn to the definition of *Dhamma (or Dharma).* The glossary stated that *Dhamma* is: "Originally, the natural condition of things, their essence, the fundamental law of their existence; then: religious truth, the doctrines and practices that make up a particular

205

religious system."[83]

As I read the definition there, the sense I gained from Buddha was that Dhamma or Dharma originally referred to the fundamental nature of reality – all reality, not Maya, but that true reality was, and still is, Dharma, the fundamental nature of things.

At that point, I realized that "All Is Well" *is* the fundamental nature of reality. That is the God-state of Being: *All is well.* Dharma, as Truth, means "All Is Well." The fundamental truth of everything is that "All Is Well."

However, at that moment, I was not feeling it.

I then experienced Buddha telling me that the reason that I was suffering was, of course, because I was holding onto desire. I acknowledged this, but said, "I don't know how to let go of the desire. Please help me."

I then heard: "Let go of the desire by knowing that all is well." I realized that choosing to believe and to trust that all is well is the same as choosing non-attachment, and that non-attachment leads to bliss, which of course, is the same as the state of "All is well."

I laughed with delight.

This is the "simple" path to Enlightenment: let go of the desire by knowing that all is well. The full circle is: choosing non-attachment by knowing that all is well, then letting go of the desire, and non-attachment leads to bliss, which is the same as being in that state in which all is well.

This "simple" path to Enlightenment often feels anything *but* easy. And yet this is the secret – just do it, and then do it again, realizing that the true and fundamental nature of reality is "All Is Well."

I had been experiencing the truth of that statement through the stresses of traveling to and through New York City. When I'm there, I'm constantly looking for trees – feeling very much not at home without greenery and nature. I also did not know how to navigate

---

[83] Armstrong, Karen, *Buddha,* (New York: Penguin Books), 2001, p. 202.

around New York very easily, being unfamiliar with it, so I found it very helpful to be mindful of "All Is Well." (And yes, New Yorkers can be friendly! Apparently, that is their true Dharma.) The really amazing truth is that, when we choose to acknowledge this fundamental basis of reality, life becomes a flow of love and joy.

I almost feel as though the name of the Divine is actually "All Is Well." It reminds me of my experience in African-American churches where the pastor will often say, "God is good," and the congregation responds, "All the time," then the pastor says, "All the time," and the congregation responds, "God is good."

May you discover the blissful, peaceful, fruitful and freeing state of "All Is Well" all the time!

Fall, 2014

Is Anything Supernatural?

For the past few weeks, I have been learning and practicing Falun Gong. Falun Gong, or Falun Dafa, is a philosophy and a practice of meditative spiritual and physical exercises which originated in China. Thanks to Master Li Hongzhi, who brought this "self-cultivation practice of the Buddha school" to the masses for free, it is now practiced by millions of people around the world.[84]

One of the exercises of Falun Gong is called, "Reinforcing Supernatural Powers." When I first saw that name in the online video, I thought, "Way to tempt our egos to seek supernatural abilities! I have no need for that ego-desire."

After a little over two weeks of watching the video and

---

[84] Please go to: http://www.falundafa.org/ although, I strongly recommend finding a local teacher to work with you in person, if possible.

practicing the exercises, I found myself thinking, "What does supernatural mean, anyway? In this post-modern, scientific age, how can we define anything as being supernatural? Is anything supernatural?"

Well, no sooner had I asked these questions, than I began to receive answers (a fact that might be considered supernatural enough in its own right!).

First, what I heard was:

"Something supernatural cannot be limited by the five senses."

Next, I heard:

"Something supernatural cannot be limited by the laws of nature."

Later, I checked dictionary.reference.com for definitions of "supernatural," and the two key points I saw there are: 1) that anything supernatural is "unexplainable by natural law or phenomena," and 2) that anything supernatural exists "outside the natural order."[85]

So, the definition I received fits well with the standard Western cultural definitions of 'supernatural.'

In addition, the definition I received clarifies the concept even more with the point: "cannot be limited by the five senses." Also, the definition I received focuses not on explanation of its character, but on delineating the lack of limits on the character of what is supernatural.

The type of answer I received confirms for me the nature of my source, that is, Ascended Masters, as it seems to me that only someone who has had experience with supernatural abilities (i.e., Ascended Masters) would define it by what cannot limit these abilities.

---

[85] http://dictionary.reference.com/

On dictionary.reference.com, there are also quotes "from the web" using the word "supernatural." The one that intrigued me was the saying: "Human beings come into the world with a predisposition to believe in supernatural phenomena." I thought, well, if it's on the web, hopefully I can find it.

My search led me immediately to a fascinating article published online by the American Psychological Association: "A Reason to Believe,"[86] by Beth Azar. The most intriguingly relevant statement I found in the article was this:

"People also have a bias for believing in the supernatural, says Barrett. In his work, he finds that children as young as age 3 naturally attribute supernatural abilities and immortality to "God," even if they've never been taught about God, and they tell elaborate stories about their lives before they were born, what Barrett calls "pre-life."

I believe the implications of these remarks are extraordinary, and too much to consider in our scope here, but, the essential concept I would like to glean from these remarks is that, even at young ages, our consciousness not only believes in the supernatural, but also evidences a possibility of consciousness going beyond the limits of nature and the five senses.

One reason that I find this consciousness of the supernatural in young children fascinating is that, secondly, when I was meditating and asked if anything is supernatural, the answer that came to me was,

"Yes, consciousness."

Please think about this with me for a moment: perhaps unlike our brains, what happens in our minds cannot be limited by the five

[86] American Psychological Association, "A Reason to Believe," by Beth Azar, December 2010, Vol. 41, No. 11, p. 52, published here: http://www.apa.org/monitor/2010/12/believe.aspx .

senses. We can think about Plato and philosophy, or the benefits of various economic systems, or how it feels emotionally to fall in love, none of which have anything to do with the five senses. Certainly, a 3 year-old talking about life before they were born is sharing a consciousness that goes way beyond the limits of the 5 senses as well as the laws of nature.

There are many accounts of children having these experiences – for instance, remembering past lives. About the same week that I received this meditative insight, I saw a teaser for a story online that referred to a young child saying, "Daddy remember that time we died...." – it turns out this was a posting on Reddit.com, where parents and others shared the "creepiest" things children have said. That site actually includes many stories that could be attributed to children referring to past lives, to ghosts, and to loved ones who have passed on, with some verification of the authenticity of some of the people and experiences that children "knew."[87]

Unfortunately, not many people in our culture are educated to believe in the truth of these experiences, so our children generally have no one helping them with their experiences of consciousness and reality. Many of us have similar stories to share about our own children, or our own childhood (or both!).

Also, our minds exist beyond natural laws, or the "laws of nature" such as entropy and gravity. Our minds, or our consciousness, may seem limited by the brain, but in the general course of the day, our consciousness can do virtually anything, from imagining the potential for life on Mars to solving complex math formulas to composing music, to dreaming of achieving our life's greatest goals, to writing fiction and poetry, to describing what we see with words that go beyond the physical description to capture the emotional and spiritual

---

[87] While I have been unable to find the original page, this page has a few relevant stories:
http://www.reddit.com/r/AskReddit/comments/105ptd/parental_units_of_reddi
t_whats_the/

elements of what we see.

Our brains, and therefore our minds may be slightly limited by the laws of nature at times, but by-and-large, consciousness is not. Consciousness can be conscious of anything. Intuitive, emotional, theoretical, scientific, or interpersonal forms of consciousness exist that are in no way limited by the laws of nature.

Consciousness is supernatural.

Consciousness is the one aspect of the universe that is not limited by the laws of nature. That is why miracles can occur. That is why we are able to create our own realities to a large degree. That's why hypnotherapy can work. That's why meditation can literally transport us to another world. That's why people can have highly developed intuition and psychic abilities. That's why each of us "knows" things sometimes, such as having a "gut feeling," without knowing how or why we know these things.

Consciousness is one aspect of the Higher Power we seek; isn't it good news that we already have it?

So, just in case you like to think of yourself as a walking, talking miracle; you truly are. Or, if you would *like* to be a walking, talking miracle, you are able to be!

Consciousness is supernatural and unlimited; as Conscious Beings filled with the power of love, we have the power to change ourselves, and the world.

So be it! Aum and Amen.

211

CHAPTER SEVENTEEN: LIVING THE "I AM" PRESENCE

Summer, 2014

A One-Week Experiment in Living the "I AM" Presence:

The Fullness of "I AM"

When one is a student on the path to Self-Realization, one may be taught to repeat the affirmation, "I AM" as an affirmation that we are One with the Divine Self. When I first began meditating over 18 years ago, and I would try to think this affirmation in my head during meditation, I merely struggled with the idea that I could be in any way connected with the Divine. The focus for me, early on, was often still on self.

Over the years, I became more aware of Higher Self, as the brow chakra became more fully energized, and then as the crown chakra unfolded the beautiful lotus petals.

With my Enlightenment Vision, I became more aware of the presence of the Divine within me. The wonderfully helpful affirmation was given to me, "The very real presence of God is within me." (Alternative version: "The very real presence of Love is within me.")

Over time and with devotion and practice, I began to focus on the "I AM" of the Divine Self, instead of the "I am" of the small self.

This week, I decided to practice the "I AM" as a mantra – all day – in order to empower myself to live in the "I AM" consciousness, and for the very mundane reason that I could then speak about it at my meditation meetup this coming Sunday night. I decided to *live* the "I AM;" that is, to practice the Presence.

Eventually, when meditating on the "I AM," I came to awareness of the fullness of the "I AM." In other words, while meditating on the words, "I AM," the conscious awareness that I began to experience is that the "I AM" is in everything and everyone. So the "I AM" became, in my mind, everything and everyone around me as well as the fullness of the universe and beyond.

This was not just a rational, conceptual experience, but also to some degree a mystical experience of the "I AM" in everyone and everything. When one experiences this oneness, along with it comes this beautiful energy of unconditional love and affection.

There is no limit to the "I AM" presence. The truth is I AM. All else follows. I AM is all there is. We are part of the great I AM of God, the great I AM of the universe. You are, we are, we are all I AM. Everything that is, is I AM.

How beautiful it is to be part of the vast expanse of I AM.

In this state, one is aware, as an observer, of one's thoughts/mind, and one is aware of the outside world of others, including plants, animals, and inanimate objects from a state of oneness.

One is also aware of higher intentions/higher consciousness relative to the present moment - or what is needed in the Now for the highest good - intuitive knowing of selfless purpose and Presence.

Because the focus is on the Divine Beingness, practicing the "I AM" as a mantra can lead to instantaneous rejoicing; the energy of overflowing joy can bubble up inside, along with a multi-hued sense of gratitude for the Divine Beingness within oneself, within the world around one, within other people, and within other beings.

One begins to see oneself as no longer separate from anyone or anything else. I admit - I have not yet fully arrived at the ability to maintain that consciousness, but, perhaps oddly enough, I began experiencing it more with animals and trees.

For instance, one day as I drove into the parking area where I live, some birds flew out of the way, and I felt keenly connected to them and their experience of the potential threat of an approaching vehicle, as well as sheer gratitude for their being and acting as they did. The other day, I was driving by the edge of Rock Creek Park just north

213

of Washington, DC, into the suburban Maryland surrounding streets and homes, when I saw a fawn (Bambi spots and all), run towards the road, and then suddenly stop, with this look of terror in its whole being - body posture and all. I slowed my car in case it did run in front of me on the road, but fortunately it turned around and ran away from the road. I felt a profound sense of empathic connection with the adorable little deer.

The "I AM" is in the fawn, in the birds, in the trees, in the grass, in ants – yes, everything. That's what is meant by the classical Western theological term, "omnipresence."[88] But knowing that term mentally and conceptually is different from mystically sensing union to the point of actually and energetically sharing consciousness with other aspects of the "I AM" outside ourselves.

The Fullness of I AM invites us into this reality from the perspective of other beings, even other objects. The other day, as I was focused on the "I AM," I was washing an ear of corn in the sink, and I became aware, from the ear of corn's perspective of the slightly rough way I was handling it to rub off the threads of corn silk. That was such a momentary glimpse in which I actually felt my hands holding "I AM" as an ear of corn. I think I pulled out of that consciousness immediately because I felt so surprised and disconcerted by having my consciousness exist inside an ear of corn, sharing its sentience.

Yes, I had a momentary doubt about the experience, with that moment of judgment that maybe I was "crazy"! However, if we truly believe the "I AM" is in everything, then sentient consciousness is in everything, and it is possible to experience this consciousness -

---

[88] One of my favorite, funny, and inspirational professors at Vanderbilt Divinity School was Dr. David Buttrick, who objected to the idea that "God was somehow in my smell sneaker." From the mystical perspective, the smelly part is an aspect of the duality of Maya, and yet, God's presence in and through the smelly sneaker is very real as energy, intention, and consciousness, for without Divine Presence as energy and intention, even a sneaker would cease to exist!

214

anywhere, and everywhere, in ourselves, and in other beings.

What moves me, though, is the profound sense of gratitude, love, and joy we can experience through practicing the Presence by repeating the mantra: "I AM."

When we live the "I AM," we rise above ourselves beyond our mind/mental limits of consciousness, to an awareness of self/Self/and Over Self. That is: mind/soul/Divine Spirit. The three become One. (I am sensing that I just channeled this teaching, and I sense that this may be the incarnation of "Trinity" in human beings.)

I have read some similar ideas recently, although I don't remember where. Lately, I have been led to read snippets in different books that describe for me what's happening with my consciousness. I love it - the "I AM" comes to me in written form after coming to me in embodied forms.

I invite you to practice the "I AM" as a mantra, allowing it to expand your awareness, preferably in connection with an ongoing devotional meditation practice. Please know that your awareness may expand throughout the Universe, as well as outside the universe. The "I AM" is everywhere, and as we become aware of our Oneness, we become both profoundly empty, as well as profoundly expanded in our consciousness.

Living the I AM, Practicing the Presence, Part 2

This week, I have been endeavoring to repeat the mantra, "I AM," as a way of raising my consciousness. Each day, I have found myself doing well in some moments, and then "dropping down," as I think of it, out of crown chakra awareness into the mental world of setting goals, feeling attached to those goals, and then experiencing feelings around the challenges of accomplishing those goals, especially when other people are involved with some of the challenges. These challenges can be simple events like another driver pulling in front of me with their car at a traffic circle when they did not have the right of way (a difficult and potentially dangerous situation).

When one maintains the "I AM", one realizes one's oneness with others, but when one drops the "I AM", one may be tempted to feel frustrated, or to feel fear, or even to judge. I have not yet managed to stay continually in the elevated consciousness of I AM, yet I have become extremely sensitized to being *out* of that consciousness – which is helpful as well.

So, practicing "I AM" as a mantra has helped me become so aware of having higher consciousness, that when I have "dropped out of it," I have felt so very upset with myself. As the week progressed, I just felt more and more upset with myself, which is a form of dropping out of the I AM as well, because we are part of the I AM, and judging ourselves or failing to love ourselves or just feeling bad about ourselves lowers our vibration as well.

I even had a discussion with someone, thinking that maybe I needed another teacher - an earthly one, not just the lovely Ascended Masters who usually teach me. Well, I finally realized that the person with whom I was speaking could teach me *about things (good things, like self-mastery techniques, but still - things)*, but not necessarily empower me to attain Self-Realization. Instead, I became more aware of the importance of cultivating love, peace, and bliss within myself, because those are keys to Self-Realization.

And yet I was not feeling peaceful, nor as loving as I would like, because I felt unhappy with myself about not accomplishing some of my goals, and because my consciousness kept dropping down out of the I AM. I also had lingering self-doubts after the conversation with the teacher.

I was thinking that maybe I was being delusional to believe that I could achieve Self-Realization on my own (without an earthly teacher, complete with official, authenticated "lineage"), and instead, in my case, "just" being taught by the Ascended Masters. ... I was pretty busy doubting myself.

Finally, the morning I wrote this, as I meditated and prayed, the intuition came to me that when one pursues the path of Self-Realization within the material world, without being able to withdraw and spend all of one's time in meditation and spiritual disciplines, then one's path is more indirect rather than a straight path, similar to the approach taken when sailing a boat.

When one sails, one holds the intention of going directly in a certain direction, but it is virtually impossible to sail directly straight in one direction and to get to that destination, unless the wind is perfect for going that particular direction at that particular time, and stays that way! Instead, one usually has to tack back-and-forth across the wind, setting what becomes essentially a zigzag course.

Similarly, when one holds the clear intention of going directly to Self-Realization, but one lives in the world, one has to alternate focus between Self-Realization and worldly goals. Until one becomes established permanently in the Self-Realized, or God-Realized state, one just zigzags in the right direction, often feeling a little off-course while still making progress. I was so grateful for receiving this intuition; it was a gift of divine grace inviting me to stop being so hard on myself.

During my meditation time, I also sensed that Buddha wanted me to read something in his book that I keep next to me when I meditate.[89] So, I picked up the book, praying that I would open it to the part that I needed, and sure enough, the story of Buddha's life to which I opened the book was about Buddha rejecting not one but two teachers, and then going off on his own to seek Enlightenment.

I believe Buddha was telling me to pursue Self-Realization "on my own", in the sense that I did not need an earthly teacher; that the Ascended Masters as my teachers more than adequately suffice!

I realized that what I experience as God in me, that elevated consciousness, the unconditional love for self and others, the peace,

---

[89] Karen Armstrong, *Buddha*, pp. 61-65.

the joyfulness, all of this is part of realizing God within my Self. I had even, a few weeks ago, felt as though I had momentarily sensed "this Atman is Brahman" as the Hindu expression goes. That dissolution of all of the self that is not Self allows one to realize that one is Self - just pure Spirit.

And then, another gift today: my lovely friend who is a follower of Meher Baba sent me two quotes from Meher Baba, and while both were helpful to me, one fit perfectly my need at this time:

"Nothing is ever written on you -- but on your mind. You, the soul, remain untarnished. Good and bad, everything is written on your mind. When the impressions go, then all is wiped out. Mind sees the soul -- this is illumination. When good and bad are written off the mind, mind sees the soul. Mind then tries to become one with the soul -- this is Realization.

Mind seeing the soul means you seeing God. But mind does not become you, you being God; mind must merge in the soul. When mind merges in soul, then you are God-Realized." [90]

I read that and realized that all of my struggles with every time I let my consciousness drop down to the level of mere mind did not matter - because it was only an experience that affected my mind - it had not damaged my soul in some way, the way I must have been subconsciously imagining.

I felt forgiven and set free to pursue my path with more self-love and acceptance. Of course, self-love and self-acceptance are essentials for us in order to be able to love and accept others. Instead of beating myself up, I could just rejoice in the brief moments in which I felt closer to having my mind merge with soul. I AM going to rejoice in those moments.

---

[90] Avatar Meher Baba, *Lord Meher*, online version, p. 1892

I AM. This is true of all of us. The more we live the awareness of I AM, the closer we come to merging the mind with the soul. Now, that is something worth practicing!

Day 3 of Living the "I AM" Presence

Today, as I began to practice the "I AM" as a mantra, I became aware that the essence of I AM is to bless. The awareness in my head became that, if I AM going to be I AM, then I exist to bless others. In other words, the activity of I AM in this world is blessing.

As I AM, my purpose is to bless others. When we live the "I AM," there is no need to be concerned about whether or not we will be blessed, because the focus is continually on blessing others in our mental level, but the larger presence of I AM is also always intending blessing for us as well.

In the "I AM," there is no need to worry. In the "I AM," there is no need for fear.

Existing for others is a blessing, for as we bless, so are we also blessed. To discover one's identity as someone who blesses others can take a while to develop. I dropped that consciousness for a moment last night, while walking home very late from the DC metro, having walked over 10 miles yesterday, and feeling a little tired. Nonetheless, I also felt very light and energized, because I had not eaten much food (I know that sounds counterintuitive - but I had been at a spiritual event for several hours, imbibing spiritual food.[91]) Even so, I had a

---

[91] The term spiritual food refers to the life force energy – energy with a high spiritual vibration that literally keeps us alive. This energy has various names in different religious traditions and spiritual practices: chi, prana, living water, Logos, the Bread of Life, the Word, etc. For instance, this is to what Jesus referred when he said that one "does not live by bread alone, but by every Word that proceeds from the mouth of God."

moment of dropping the smile of peace and bliss, only to see a young man, a stranger, smile and nod at me in the parking garage.

Oh, I did regret that moment of failing to respond energetically with a nod, a smile. Maybe I was somewhat smiling, or energetically glowing; I don't know. Nodding is not a customary habit for me, but smiling is certainly becoming more of a habit. I exist to bless - everyone. Everyone is precious, so I regret not recognizing another precious soul – even a stranger at night - with a symbolic affirmation.

I know that we are taught to be wary of strangers, especially at night, especially if we are women encountering men. However, his smile was clearly a soul smile, and we all would do well to smile to one another from the depths of our souls to the depths of other people's souls. On that level, we are one.

When we are one with the energy of blessing, people (and animals) intuitively feel it, and some may even see it.

From my experience, it seems that the more we exist to bless others, the more blessed we become. Affirming "I AM" lightly with our mind allows us to be aware of a larger circle of reality, without engaging the left-brain, goal-oriented mind that becomes so easily attached to outcomes based on our behaviors.

I AM. I exist to bless, and I AM one with the "I AM" who blesses me; therefore, I exist in a state of trust. As I trust I AM, I allow peace to pervade my being. As I remain "affectionately detached,"[92] I allow life to flow and to unfold as is needed, rather than controlling it with my ego.

I empty myself and I AM. I AM and I exist to bless.

---

[92] Ravindra Kumar, *Kundalini for Beginners,* (St. Paul: Llewellyn Publications), 2000, p. 10.

CHAPTER EIGHTEEN: THE TAO
OF BLESSING OTHERS

The Tao of Divine Presence

One day, I paused for a moment of meditation, and am grateful to say that I felt Divine connection. As I was lifting up a question, something along the lines of: "Why are we sometimes asked to do such difficult things," the answer that I received from the Divine Presence was this:

"I ask nothing of you for myself. I ask for your [plural - meaning for all human beings] sake. I need nothing. It is my creation that needs redemption, and so I ask you to be my Presence, and without asking anything of anyone, bring redemption to my offspring. How else will they know my love, unless you love them for me? How else will they receive, without having to give in equal exchange, unless you give to them unconditionally? How else will they heal and become whole, unless you forgive them? How else will they know to find me, unless they see me in you? Give, without asking to receive, for I will provide for you. Do, without asking for it to be done for you, for I will do and be with and for you. You have no true needs that will remain unmet, for you are with me. Choose my Presence within you, and all your needs will be fulfilled. Focus then, your life each day, on the needs of others, for that is the Divine Tao, the Divine Purpose, the Divine Path, the Way of Divine Presence upon the earth. So be it."

October 8, 2014

The Tao as a Way of Being

At the beginning of September, a few friends and I started a new interfaith spiritual community: the Self-Realization Community (not to be confused with the Self-Realization Fellowship, established by Paramahansa Yogananda). Lovely people have been drawn to be a part of it, including children, who add so much to the main goal: embodying Divine Presence individually and together.

One of my challenges as the spiritual leader of the community has been figuring out what to do for readings. Because I came out of a background of serving churches as a Christian minister, I was accustomed to having four Biblical scriptures from which to select each Sunday, out of what is called the Revised Common Lectionary.

Without this tangible guide as to what to read each week, for the Self-Realization Community (SRC), I pray to be intuitively guided as to the selection of readings. Generally, I find readings from among the many spiritual books I already have, or occasionally from books which present themselves to me as new opportunities for learning and sharing. The topics for the messages (sermons) for each Sunday also have to come through intuition. I trust the leading of the Divine through life events on an ongoing basis to provide topics as they are needed – of course, I do have to pray and ask for them!

Well, I decided for the third topic to be "Divine Will," but then I had to decide, hopefully led by Spirit, which readings to use. I chose mainly a number of short sayings out of the book: *Jesus and Lao Tzu: The Parallel Sayings.* I figured that if both of these enlightened teachers agreed on something, then it was definitely a guide for how we are to live our lives.

The only problem was that I could not seem to intuit how to express how we are to discern what divine will is in any given moment. It's not that ideas haven't previously come to me; it's that the ideas and intuitions just weren't flowing.

Finally, I had a spiritual breakthrough, but only because I had a breakthrough with a seeming blockage in my personal life.

That block in my personal life was income. All of my income from four different sources had been delayed in coming to me. One day, there were literally four checks that I "should" have already received.

When I realized that even the fourth check was delayed, I finally asked the Divine Universe why these checks were delayed. The answer I received was this: The universe needed to get my attention, to let me know that as long as I delayed becoming who I am meant to be, the blessings from being who I am created to be would be delayed as well.

And then I had an "Ah-ha!" moment. I realized that Divine Will is not about something we do or don't do; Divine Will is about *Being* who we are meant to be.

I had been accustomed to the Christian tradition, in which one talks about Divine Will as something we are supposed to do, as well as things we are supposed to avoid doing. As a matter of fact, as I drove to the spiritual community to share this message that Sunday, I saw a church sign which read: "Stop sinning and walk with God." (In other words, salvation by doing.)

From my understanding, the Jewish tradition also focuses on obeying or "doing" the Law. On the interfaith spiritual path, we tend to talk about what we are doing on the path, or about moving forward on the path, or about what is happening on our spiritual paths. All of these approaches focus on doing, rather than Being.

But the truth is that the Tao is not about doing; the Tao is about Being.

The Tao is about a way of being. The Tao is about being who we are meant to be.

When we attain a higher state of consciousness that allows us to Be Divine Presence, then we are fully doing the "Will of God." Our doing flows from our Being. Being leads to doing, not vice-versa.

Achieving enlightenment or Buddha-Consciousness or Christ-Consciousness is about Being our Higher Selves. The Reign of God is within us because the Reign of God is who we are when we are in alignment with our Higher Selves.

Who we are matters. We are meant to become Self-Realized. We are meant to live as our Higher Selves, rather than as merely our ego selves. Who we are matters; who we are Being, ego self or Higher Self, determines whether or not we are fulfilling Divine Will.

May you be who you are meant to become. May you discover within yourself the Tao of Being.

Nov 13, 2014

A Morning of Ascension with the Masters

My mother passed away May 31st, 2014. Since she passed away, I have much more easily been able to perceive and to appreciate the beauty of her soul. I appreciate her love and miss her – especially her older, sweeter self, very much.

With my mother's passing, this left a small inheritance for my older sister, older brother and myself. Not a lot, but just a touch of grace for me as a fifty-six-year-old who had depleted her savings and had spent many of the last six years significantly under-earning relative to the expenses of twenty-first century life, especially in the Washington, DC, area.

Interestingly, the disbursement of the inheritance kept getting delayed, and yet, I needed it as a way of supporting myself for a few months while starting the spiritual community. I knew why it was delayed in earthly terms, but I did not know why in spiritual terms. I finally asked God and the Higher-Ups. It became clear to me that I needed to prioritize healing my relationships with my siblings before receiving the money.

Without going into details as to why this seemed difficult, suffice it to say that such a possibility looked and felt challenging to me. Yet, I was shown that my "Self" as a healer needed to choose this healing process for my siblings and for myself.

Within 24 hours of when I chose to hold the intention of the possible healing of my relationships with my sister and brother, my brother called me, and as we talked, our relationship began to heal, and indeed has done so.

I was shown that I had a deep issue to heal within myself – lifetime ego stuff – before my relationship with my sister could heal.

As part of communicating with siblings about our inheritance, I received a text message from my sister that initiated a painful healing process. This process included bringing up my family of origin wounds as well as my own ego-dysfunction that has plagued me since I was a small child trying to cope with my place in the family, in a world where we moved about half-way around it every one or two years.

This was an extremely painful emotional healing process for me. I had to pray and practice some spiritual exercises in order to begin to connect with God and the Higher-Ups, because I felt so disappointed in realizing my old patterns of inner dysfunctions which had been revealed to me. I was determined to release the old patterns, to heal, and to re-connect with God somehow, even though I felt so unworthy.

I sat to meditate, and ascended, at first to the feet of the masters. I literally kissed their feet in gratitude for being there, and in gratitude for who they are and all they have done. And then, I realized that I did not know where to sit. The Masters were sitting around the circle, on chairs as it were. I couldn't sit in the middle of the circle

225

We Are

One

where I had been kneeling, because I knew I did not belong in the center – the center of attention if you will. So, I sat in the circle with them – in a chair around the edge of the circle, feeling very hesitant about belonging there – very unworthy. So, I looked around the circle to see my Beloved Ascended Ones, to whom I pray every day for wisdom, love, blessings, teachings, and companionship.

At first, it was as though I was too afraid to look at them directly, so I just "saw" Mother Mary and Jesus because they are so comforting to me. But then I saw Paramahansaji, and he was sitting there very relaxed, with his hands on his knees, and he smiled at me his big smile, welcoming me. I felt so much better. Then, I saw Buddha, who did look at me, the kind of look that makes one desire never to have any ego-consciousness again.

Then, I realized that I could directly look at each one of my Beloved Ascendeds. I looked at Mother Mary, and she is so loving. She told me to purify my intentions, to be of pure intention. She vibrates with such purity. She said that is why she is called a virgin.

I looked at High Priest Melchizedek, and he told me to

"Grow up, child, and be strong."

I looked at Lady Kwan Yin, and she told me,

"Accept my people."

She was referring to people from China and other parts of Asia, from whom I had felt so disconnected linguistically and culturally, in part because most of my life had been focused on Africa and America – I hadn't stretched my focus that much to Asia.[93] (Ego separates; love unites.)

I looked at Mary Magdalene, and she explained that she is

"Empathy, connection with people through empathic love."

That is her essence, and what she represents.

---

[93] I had not focused much on South America, either, until recently. One of the reasons that I love living in the DC area is that one encounters people from all over the world, making it easier to learn about many different places and peoples.

I looked at Master Usui,[94] and asked how I could become a really great healer, and then realized that I wanted to ask that of Jesus, whom I experience as the greatest healer of all. Jesus told me,

"Discipline the mind to know that all is well.
All will be well."

I turned to Master Lao Tzu, and asked to find wisdom. Master Lao Tzu told me,

"Wisdom is everywhere and in everyone and everything. Find the inner wisdom, for that is the Tao."

I felt complete with these messages, and returned to my body.

February and April, 2015

The Physics of Co-Creating "Reality"

Long ago, I perceived that there are three aspects of "reality." First, there is the Ontological, which is what is Really Real, or the very nature of God. God's ontological nature emanates into the universe as the essence or Spirit of God – the Aum. Second, there is the Existential, or the temporary aspects of "reality" which appear as the cosmic illusion, or Maya – what we experience in life. And third, there is the teleological – or purpose of life in this Universe, which is to return to a state of Union with God.

Also a few years ago, I received the intuition that God's energy in creation is the *wave form* of that energy, and that matter is comprised

---

[94] The founder of Reiki in Japan.

of what "blips" into existence as particles. In other words, matter is simply an expression of the Light of God, condensed into particle form.

The dual nature of light, that is, both particle and wave, creates the fundamental nature of Maya, or the dual nature of "reality" in this universe. Maya may be described as the illusion of "reality" in this universe, because it emanates from God as a wave of light, but then becomes transformed into temporary particles of matter. The Light of God is real; the particles are the temporary form of existence which is transient and changeable in nature.

Recently, I received this intuition:

"When you're one with the wave, you're one with creation."

In other words, when we remain calmly one with waves of Divine energy, we are one with the state of Divine creation. This state is commonly referred to as: *going with the flow.* Or, this state of Oneness with the Divine wave of energy may be called *"the flow state,"* or *"grace,"* or *"co-creation."*

Also, *this flow state is the Tao, in which All Is Well.*

Resistance to the energy wave of "what is" creates particles. In other words, if we resent, or block the flow of energy instead of remaining one with the Divine wave flow, we create particles of resistance. These particles create karmic twins that match their resonance. In this way, our inward resistance in the form of thought particles creates particles of energy outside ourselves that mirror our own blockage of the flow of Divine energy.

By our own resistance to the flow of Life, we karmically create lower vibrations through particles of resistance that appear outside of us. When we resist the Divine flow of energy, we create "reality" that matches our resistance. What is created thus matches our fears, our

230

hurts, or our desires, rather than matching the Divine state of grace.

By contrast, acceptance of "what is" enables us to be one with the Divine wave of energy which is creating Divine Will. This is called "going with the flow," which is commonly recognized as beneficial.

The reason that going with the flow is beneficial is that *acceptance* harmonizes with the wave of divine creation, and so the only particles emitted by us in this state of grace concretize Divine Will. In other words, our conscious act of acceptance maintains our unity with the Divine wave of Creation, which then results in our co-creating particles which will harmonize with Divine Designs for life.

And there we have it: we can either be and remain part of the wave of God's consciousness in the universe, co-creating in harmony with Divine Will, which results in our living in a constant state of grace (in which All Is Well), or we can be in a state of resistance, which results in our remaining in states of struggle and lack of fulfillment of our Divine Selves.

This is why the quiet mind or observer mind of the meditative state is so helpful; it simply goes with the flow.

The choice is ours: learn to meditate and to achieve oneness with the constant flow of Divine Loving Consciousness, co-creating Divine Will all around us and in us and through us, or separating ourselves and creating particles of Maya which dance to their own tune, and which fail to harmonize with the grander schemes of Life in this Universe.

May we learn to flow with the dance of Life, harmonizing as One with the flow of Unconditional Love, which alone creates the third aspect of "reality": the *Teleological*. The Teleological aspect of reality is the ultimate goal of this universe of Maya: complete wholeness, healing, and union with that Divine original state of Being which is the Tao of Love, and Peace, and Bliss.

The ultimate *teleos* of creation is for all of us to be One in this state of Being in which *All Is Well*.

ॐ

Economy of Blessing

In the fall of 2014, God brought me this lesson by first asking me to live it. Living it is amazing; the more we bless others, the more blessed we become.

The Divine is about giving and blessing. We are also therefore in alignment with the Divine Will when we are giving and blessing. If we would become divine, then we need to be giving and blessing, with no expectation of anything in return.

It is possible to have an Economy of Blessing. That is God's Economy: where people are simply, purely, and fully-consciously focused on the blessing of others, blessing all life, even insects.[95]

Blessing others creates the natural order of God's Economy in the world.

Most life forms naturally do not know this as we come into this world, and so we take what we need in order to survive, even if it means taking it from another life form. We also often take what we want in order to experience pleasure. As humans, we generally experience ourselves as seeking to survive first and foremost, and in economic terms, that means we create an economy of taking, which is our effort at economic survival.

However, spiritually speaking, being human constitutes an invitation to arise from the economy of taking to the Economy of Blessing.

Lest we feel too threatened by this idea, we need to know that the Economy of Blessing is not just about giving everything away. Just

---

[95] Blessing insects does not mean that we never kill them; that might indeed be necessary for our survival and well-being, however, appreciating them as life forms is essential, since Life in everyone and everything is a gift of Divine Presence.

232

as giving is part of the Economy of Blessing, so also receiving is part of the Economy of Blessing.

There is a contrast of beliefs between the economy of taking and the Economy of Blessing. The economy of taking believes that one has to be strong, dominant, hard-working and also worthy in order to "receive." In the economy of taking, this is called earning rather than receiving. However, the only way we can be said to "earn" anything is out of the illusion of our separateness of being, both from God, and from one another.

By contrast, the Economy of Blessing means that, in order to receive, one exists in a state of grace, which is gratitude, faith, deep trust, unconditional blessing, and that deep connection which may be called Oneness. Or, in order to receive in the Economy of Blessing, one simply has to be in a state of need.

In the Economy of Blessing, everyone who has a Higher Self, no matter how separate one may feel or in fact be from that Higher Self, has an automatic invitation to receive Divine Blessing. All Life has an invitation to receive Divine Blessing.

Sometimes we are energetically very far from the Energy/Intentions of our Higher Selves, largely because we are so far from the flow of energy which is Oneness. At those times, we most need the Economy of Blessing.

The economy of taking, or survival economy, arises because of our ego's sense of separation from God and from one another.

The knowledge of good and evil (Adam & Eve eating the metaphorical apple in the Garden of Eden) originates through this perception of separation. This sense of separation leads, in turn, to perceiving the Universe as having the dualistic nature of good and evil. However, this dualism is false – just part of the Illusion of Maya.

Yet, because of this sense of separation, we believe that we need to grab, to take, or to work hard in order to earn that which seems otherwise out-of-reach when we need it or want it. So, as ego selves, we focus on ourselves. We make ourselves and our own well-being our primary focus.

Again by contrast, as Higher Selves, our business is other people. Our business is other people, because God's "business" is people. God's main purpose in this Universe is to create the whole amazing variety of us and to invite and empower us to become One with the Divine Mother/Father. We can only become One with our Divine Mother/Father by accepting that we are One with each other.

Because our business is other people, one aspect of that job assignment from the Divine is to empower and bless other people's business, other people's health, and other people's economic success. That is the "new" economy of blessing: prioritizing the blessing of other people's well-being on all levels, including their career and financial success.[96]

For so long, we have been in lock-down mentality as far as what the Divine intends economically,

"But now it is being revealed around the world that God's intention is an economy of blessing."

The economy of blessing goes well beyond charity, because mere charity does not heal or create wholeness, economically or otherwise.

The economy of blessing includes generosity of sacrificial proportions, along with genuine empathic compassion. This includes concern for people's physical well-being, as in caring for the sick and the hungry, but not merely through acts of giving, but more importantly through acts of empowerment. This includes sharing all basic forms of wealth.

This is a radical economy devoted to the well-being of the "poor." This is also a radical economy of well-being which asks us to bless even those who have "more" than we appear to "have." This is a radical economy of blessing which asks us to bless even those who

---

[96] This is, of course, a very old concept. The economy of blessing can be seen in the many indigenous cooperative societies that have existed, and to some extent still exist around the earth, as well as in Judaism with the concepts of shalom, the Year of Jubilee, and much of the teachings of Old Testament prophets.

would harm us or who are clearly out-of-alignment with the Divine Will of Blessing.

Notice, if you will, that we are never asking the question, "What's in this for me?" Nor do we ask, "How will God provide for us?" We will not even answer such fear-based questions at this time. In God, there is no room for fear. In an Economy of Blessing, there is no need for fear.[97]

The Economy of Blessing is the Consciousness of God made visible through the Spirit/Energy of intending blessing for others. Energy follows intention. Divine Intention is giving, blessing, creating, sustaining. When we follow the Divine Intentions, all the energy which is needed will flow to us and through us.

God is in everyone. Therefore, our business is becoming One with God, One with one another, and blessing everyone.

When we do this, the Reign of God will be complete upon the Earth. This is the fulfilling of what Jesus meant by the kingdom of God on earth. This is Supreme Nirvana; the Garden of Eden for everyone, for this can only be achieved through states of near-Nirvana.

In Judaism, this is Tikkun Olam. Tikkun Olam refers to repairing or healing the world. This is the Will of God for this Earth.

In Islam, this is the winning of the Greater Jihad (not the lesser jihad of violent war against the "infidel"). The Greater Jihad is a non-violent spiritual concept of winning the struggle against good and evil (ego and Higher Self) within ourselves. When we win this internal struggle, we cease to fight, and become a blessing.[98]

---

[97] Please note that I was "channeling" some of these statements!

[98] Please see this beautiful explanation of jihad by Fethullah Gullen, which resonates with Self-Realization:
http://www.onislam.net/english/reading-islam/understanding-islam/ethics-and-values/444628-understanding-lesser-and-greater-jihad.html?Values=

In Lakota tradition, this is the fulfillment of the affirmation: Aho, Mitakuye Oyasin.[99]

In the Hawaiian tradition of Huna, this is the fulfilling of Aloha.[100]

This is Namaste, beautifully and poetically expressed by these words:

"I honour the place in you
Where the entire universe resides.
I honour the place in you
Of Light, Love, Truth, Peace and Wisdom.
I honour the place in you where,
When you are in that place, and I am in that place,
There is only one of us."[101]

This is the Tao: Being Blessing.

The Economy of Blessing is the origin of the Universe.
The Economy of Blessing is also the end and
fulfillment of the Universe as we know it.

So Be It. Aum. Amen. Shalom. Salaam. Aho. Aloha. Namaste.

---

[99] "All my relations," which refers to every level of reality; people, plants, animals, spirits, universe, equally, and in a circle of life.

[100] Please see: http://www.huna.org/html/deeper.html where Aloha sounds like Self-Realization.

[101] This description of Namaste can be found many places; I found these words attributed to Mahatma Gandhi on this site:

https://elanoflife.wordpress.com/category/native-american/